The Ecstasy of Gold

Friendship, Honor and Turkey Hunting, A 34 Year Journey

Bob Henderson, Jr.

Edited by Jim Casada and Julie Coolidge

Montane Press
1022 1st Street North, Suite 201
Alabaster, AL 35007

ISBN 978-0-578-62675-8

Printed in the USA.

Bob Henderson, Jr., author of The Fire Tower, has been hunting turkeys for most of his life in and around the great state of Alabama. He is a purist in sport, unwilling to kill turkeys by less than honorable means in the likes of the old pros. He currently lives in Birmingham, AL with his wife and two children. When he's not hunting, he practices dermatology in Alabaster.

Contents

INTRODUCTION

In 1997, my father and I started turkey hunting a property just outside Birmingham made up of 5,000 acres of solid, mature hardwoods and provided us the most successful turkey location we'd hunted to date, based on the number of years we hunted it and our productivity in killing turkeys there. And because it was close to home, we hunted it a lot. Though the tract was extensive, a significant portion was too hilly and steep to hunt. Double Oak Mountain ran the length of the property, with undulations and steep mountainsides carving themselves into naturally occurring, self-contained locations for hunting. One such location, which we called The Chamber, was hidden away, reachable only through significant effort by walking along the steep mountainside through thick understory until it opened up and leveled out. We often went there in the mid-mornings to sit and call and experience a phenomenon that occurred at 10:30 most mornings – the forest coming alive for 30 minutes with far-off bells and female opera-esque singing blaring over a loudspeaker from a church at the base of the mountain perhaps a mile away. Sitting there listening to the music, we'd hope, if not fantasize, that a turkey would come up in all his glory while the beautiful music resonated through the majestic forest around us. While such an event never did happen, the experience created a new dimension of turkey hunting I never before experienced; thereafter I could associate music with turkey hunting.

If you know the movie, "The Good, The Bad and The Ugly," then no doubt you're drawn to the theme song played commonly on various radio and television programs and commercials. It epitomizes the brazen ruggedness of the characters in the movie. In fact, the whole soundtrack is fantastic. When listening to one of the songs in particular, the next-to-last song on the soundtrack, "L'estasi dell'oro," or "The Ecstasy of Gold," I'm taken on a journey through a complete turkey hunt, allowing me to experience my passion most any time I want.

If you'll permit me the opportunity to connect the less than obvious, I'll take you briefly through the components of the song and then draw a parallel with a turkey hunt. The score opens with soft piano and clarinet, a subtle and mellow build until it is interrupted by a sharp cymbal to usher in a beautiful operatic female voice accompanied by the full breadth of an orchestra with drums, strings, woodwinds, and horns, proceeding in a crescendo of intensity, her voice being dominant, until a pause, as if all is lost, a sullen moment, only to have all the sounds and singing burst forth again to soothe our despair. Eventually, her singing subsides and the variability of sounds evens out into a steady tempo, heavy on the drums, climaxing in a seemingly chaotic merger of myriad sounds that suddenly cease into silence. Can you hear it?

It takes imagination, but it's all there, a complete turkey hunt. Follow the parallel: the soft sounds of the predawn darkness and anticipation are suddenly broken by the majestic sound of gobbling, his operatic voice ringing among the varied and lively musical sounds in a springtime forest, proceeding in crescendo fashion as he flies down and moves about the forest, responding to our calls, playing the game as he ought to, a game of sound not sight, until he suddenly goes quiet for a spell, which often happens during classic turkey hunts, a sullen moment which imparts heartbreak and despair, hoping it's not over, that he didn't move off or worse yet, get spooked. But when it picks back up, he again fills the forest with his music against the backdrop of various noises of birds singing, woodpeckers tapping, and owls hooting. As he works in, he often quits gobbling and our senses get overwhelmed listening to the multitude of noises such as drumming and walking in the leaves with birds still singing in the background, all becoming a bit chaotic considering the intense attention and necessary decision-making in order to be ready when he presents himself, and then with a sudden overpowering boom, all goes silent.

The following pages are actual stories I wrote about each and every turkey I shot over my life. All but one occurred in Alabama. In 1986, I was 13 years old when I killed my second turkey. I was so excited about the kill, because I had called him up and shot him while my father was lying asleep next beside me, that I jotted down the details of the hunt on a scrap piece of paper, rolled it up and stuffed it into the shell with which I had shot the turkey. And since I had kept the shell from the first turkey I killed, I did the same thing from memory about that kill and stuffed it into that shell too. The next turkey I killed, I wrote down the details, this time a bit more detailed, and rolled it up to stuff in the shell as before. And because I started a trend, I kept doing this for each turkey I shot thereafter, including the ones I missed, until I was sometimes writing extensive stories to capture the details of the hunt for such times when my memory would no longer carry me.

I'm afraid I've reached that point in my life. While I still remember bits and pieces for almost every kill, I started pulling out these stories recently and reading – much to my delight – the highs and lows of turkey hunts gone by. Though I never intended anyone else to read these stories, there's value to putting them into print; not to bolster my ego, but perhaps to present the most intimate of thoughts of a dedicated turkey hunter during the most meaningful aspects of a lifetime of hunting experiences.

Through these pages, you'll get a chance to see the thoughts of a young turkey hunter learning through experience. You'll get to watch this boy grow up, see the ideals of his pursuit change, and witness his values maturing into the likes of the old pros. You'll also witness the closest and most unlikely of friendships forged amongst the pursuit of nature's grandest subject. Some of the stories are short and routine; others are more elaborate in detail and gripping. It may be unreasonable to expect anyone to read through all these stories at one sitting, for surely such repetitive "turkey gobbles, turkey comes in, and hunter shoots turkey" would numb the interest of even the most avid of readers. But hopefully, the stories have value for reference and to pass time on rainy days.

The stories are presented in near original form with only minor edits for the most nonsensical wording and overt grammatical errors. I've kept them this way so you can hear the stories through my voice at the time and my age of their writing.

So, I invite you come along a 35-year journey, to read the intimate stories of a dedicated turkey hunter who grows up before you on the pages. With me, you'll experience the highs and lows over my turkey hunting career. You'll witness a deep friendship with my father, bound and unwavering over the decades. Perhaps, if you read on, and if you imagine, you too will too hear the music – the music of "The Ecstasy of Gold."

THE DATA

Apart from detailing the events of the kill or miss, most of the original stories also contain data about the shot including such pertinent information as gun used, shell used, time of day, distance of the shot in addition to information that everyone cares about including turkey weight and beard and spur length. Not every story has all the same information, but by and large most do. Later in my career, I quit routinely measuring beard and spur length and weight because if the turkey gobbled, then I really didn't care about those things unless the spurs were really long and sharp or beard unusually long. Some of the early stories are missing data altogether. But since I rolled all the stories up and stuffed them into the shot shells used to shoot the turkeys with from the get-go, I've got most all the shells I shot the turkeys with, which helps fill in the gaps of missing information. Thus, I have a nearly complete record of weapons and ammunition used to shoot 104 turkeys, something I'm not aware of ever being published by anybody else. I would be remiss to not present such a treasure trove in some form, which I do so here and use to explain a very troubling aspect of my turkey hunting career which you will read much about in this book. When I solicited an editor to review an early edition of this book, deep into his reading he commented bluntly about the issue saying,

> I really think you need to say something about this
> propensity for misses and what you did (or are doing)
> to correct it. There are enough incidents of crippled birds
> and uncertainty to give readers, including me, some misgivings. Mind you, I've missed my share of turkeys and then
> some, but only once to my knowledge did I cripple a bird
> and not retrieve it. There are a lot of questions here. Does
> use of older shotshells have an impact? Does use of different
> guns figure in the equation? Are you meticulously patterning
> the guns you use? Have you carefully analyzed the explanation
> for the recurrent misses?

Contemplating his suggestion, I realized I had all the data to answer his questions right there before me. Analyzing it in regards to the killing part of turkeys to include gun and shot shell used as well as distance of the shot shows a remarkably unexpected correlation that might only relate to my own idiosyncrasies, but I'm willing to bet it applies to most everyone and may explain a lot of misses that happen out there.

In 1993 I missed three turkeys, then one in 1996, and 10 others from 2000 to 2019. So I have missed 14 turkeys out of 104 times pulling the trigger. When I say "missed," I'm referring to those that I never recovered with follow-up shots. If you consider all the turkeys I missed with my initial shot, whether or not I killed them with follow-up shots, then the number is 23 misses out of 104. At first glance, that ratio is striking and disconcerting as expressed by the editor quoted above. It confirms the years of mental anguish I suffered and subsequent devotion to figuring out the reasons why and taking action to correct the problem. But the answers are in the data which, analyzing for the first time, has helped me make sense of the matter for once and for all. I wish I had performed the exercise long ago.

If I'm going to direct appropriate blame for my propensity to miss turkeys on one thing, then I'm going to place that blame squarely on me. To put it frankly, I'm not good at shooting turkeys.

In early March, 2018, before the spring turkey season began, Dad and I went to Argentina for the legendary dove shooting everyone talks about. Indeed, the experience was phenomenal. I killed 4,600 dove over the span of four days, and two of those days were half days only. As incredible as that number is, the more amazing statistic is my percentage of dove killed which approached 90 percent. Never mind that cutting a feather counted as a kill, nor did it matter if the bird was retrieved or even if it died. If your bird boy saw any evidence of a hit, your score increased by one in the kill category. So the numbers are artificial, but if you could extract the true count, I can promise I killed well over 50 percent of the dove I shot at, perhaps even 75 percent. All that is to say that I'm a good dove shooter and always have been. So why I have a tougher time with turkeys, whose heads are about the same size as a dove, and who are usually standing still, remains a mystery to me.

I think the first problem is my nerves. I get rattled when a turkey walks up to me. I mentioned in the introduction the chaotic nature of the moments just before shooting a turkey. When a gobbler comes in among the brush and trees, a good shot doesn't often present itself. And this happens in the most critical of moments, for as the turkey gets closer, he's more likely to spot you and spook. Since I shoot most of my turkeys in woods, waiting for an ideal opportunity to shoot when he stops walking and no bush or tree is in the line of fire adds difficulty. And I don't use decoys. I'm fairly certain turkeys wouldn't see me as easy if their attention was focused on a spread of decoys out front of me. I've called in so many turkeys through the years that saw me and spooked before I could get a shot, which has been almost as disconcerting as the number I've missed. In fact, I've spent a similar amount of time and mental energy over the decades analyzing the reasons why turkeys have seen me and spooked including patterns of camouflage and characteristics of set ups as I have for the reasons I missed. I've taken blinds into the woods with me many times, but I hate them. Since I don't sit on green fields with decoys, I have to tote the blinds with me on the move. I hate carrying them and trying to stick the poles into the sometimes hard and rocky ground while a turkey is out there gobbling, and sitting behind one makes the circumstance feel artificial. So I'll admit that by forgoing decoys and blinds, and sitting by green fields for that matter, I'm stacking the cards against me. I sometimes break leafed-out limbs and put them in front to help hide me, but other than that simple manipulation I have to blend into the elements by picking good trees and being as still as possible. And this gives turkeys a big advantage. Thus many turkeys have seen me through the years.

So when a turkey is coming to me through the woods, looking with all his attention for that hen who's been calling to him, weaving closer behind bushes and trees, knowing that if you can see him then he can see you, and knowing that these Alabama wild turkeys spook at the mere possibility of danger, and that I'm not always in a comfortable or ideal shooting position, sometimes twisted sideways holding a gun that's getting heavier by the second, pulling the trigger is often a spur of the moment decision knowing that the shot may not be ideal but might also be the only opportunity I get before he goes off or spooks. And for this reason, I'm often taking less than ideal shots which has led to more missed shots.

Now on to the data…

I'm a rarity of a subject to study in the art of shooting turkeys because I've used so many different guns and shells over the years. And the different gun/shell combos are so widely variable in size, power, and design including those considered modern and vintage, that analyzing their effectiveness affords rare insight into figuring out which characteristics of those guns and shells work and which don't.

Conventional wisdom holds that more powerful weaponry with tighter patterns is better for killing turkeys. The opposite has been true in my case. Of the 23 turkeys I missed (initial shots), 10 were with modern ultra-tight choked guns chambered for 3-inch or 3 ½-inch magnums to include a Mossberg 835 Ulti-Mag, Ithaca Model 37, and Winchester Model 1300 all purchased in the 1990s. In fact, if you total the misses and kills, then these supremely powered guns missed 10 of 24 turkeys. To counterpoint this paradox, I've shot 16 turkeys with vintage weapons only missing twice. The "vintage weapons" include an old Iver Johnson 12-gauge single shot, L.C. Smith 16-gauge side by side, and Fox Sterlingworth 12-gauge side by side. I often paired these vintage weapons with old paper shells for a true throwback to old. That's pretty darn good shooting for what most would consider inadequate firepower.

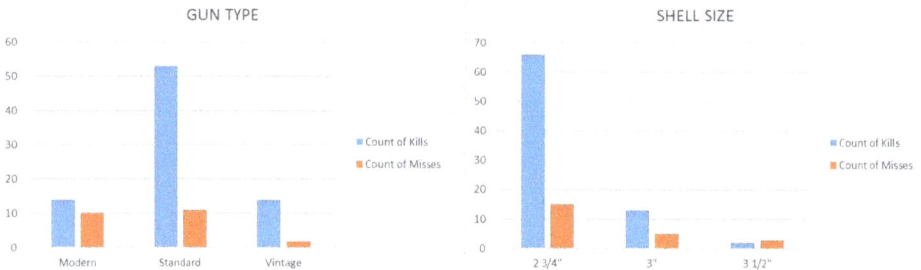

These days, turkey loads are more often sold with lighter loads resulting in higher velocities. I've never liked this trend, and my data back that sentiment up. Higher muzzle velocities do not kill turkeys more effectively. In fact, neither velocity, shot size or shell load (oz. shot) seemed to make any difference. And to complete the analysis, as expected, efficiency worsened at longer distances.

Most of my turkeys were killed with several different old Ithaca Model 37s chambered for 2 ¾ inches, most being 12 gauges and one a 16-gauge. Of these, I killed 53 of 64 with the initial shot, a respectable ratio in the likes the vintage guns.

Conventional advice by all the writers and manufactures says that killing turkeys requires a dense pattern, and the denser the better. But no one discusses at what cost. Denser patterns require more accurate shots. No doubt many of you are more accurate shots than me, and shooting turkeys distracted by decoys gives better opportunity to take an easy clean shot, but I'm apparently not that accurate and many of my shots, as discussed above, are difficult, split-second decisions in the woods. I think the reason I've missed more turkeys with the modern guns is their tight patterns. While there could be something about the nature of 3-inch or 3 ½-inch shells that contribute to missing as well, I'm going to pin the culprit on tighter patterns. It only takes one pellet to penetrate the central nervous system, that being the brain or spinal cord, to render the turkey unable to run or fly away. So why does everyone want to see numerous pellets in the kill zone when patterning a gun? Obviously the pattern can be too sparse, so a good pattern does matter, but I'm sure I've missed many turkeys because the pattern was too tight.

Now that I've taken my stand with data to back me up, there is a new shell on the market that could render the above analysis obsolete. Of the 104 turkey shots described in this book, 98 were carried out with tried and true lead shot. But several years ago I bought a box of specially loaded shells with Hevi-Shot® # 7 ½s in hopes that they would afford more pellets per shell with each pellet approximating the weight and energy of #6 lead. I did the calculations at the time, knowing the weight of each, and concluded that the load should be superior to #6 lead. Unfortunately I missed three of four turkeys I shot with them. So I ditched the shells and went back to lead exclusively. Well, now there is another lead substitute on the market that is without question far superior to lead. Tungsten Super Shot, or TSS, is 60 percent heavier than lead so that shooting #9 or #10 shot provides more effective downrange energy than #5 lead. Skipping the technical details that explain why, these TSS loads have far more pellets per ounce compared to the tried and true lead loads and are more deadly downrange too. So whereas I stated above that this new load could render my stance in regards to the inferiority of higher powered, tighter choked guns obsolete, I'm not convinced it will matter. Super tight chokes with TSS loads will be just as tight as lead, if not tighter and you will still miss a turkey if the shot isn't accurate. But if we buck conventional wisdom, then there is a remarkable advantage to using them that is likely to dramatically reduce missed shots, at least for me anyhow. When patterning TSS in multiple guns with multiple chokes this past spring, I found that modified chokes patterned both wider and denser than lead loads through full chokes. The key there is wider. Wider patterns are more forgiving when shots aren't so accurate, and that will be a remarkable advantage for me going forward indeed.

To round out the data, because it's all there to be looked at, the following chart groups all shots according to time of day. Not unexpectedly, mornings were best and evenly distributed through mid-morning, but I've had a little success later in the days too.

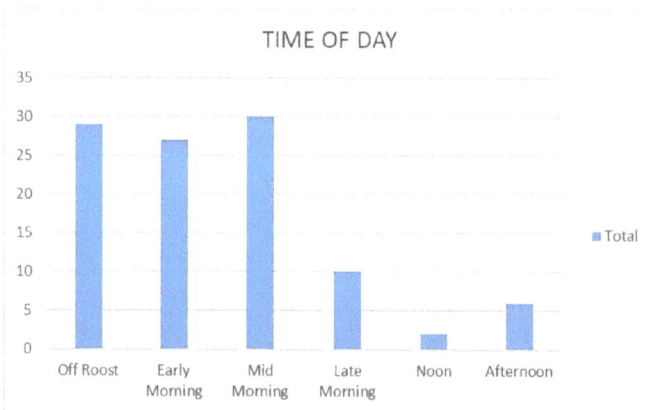

	Time of Day	Gun	Gauge	Shell	Shell Size	Shot Size	oz Shot	Velocity	Distance	Notes
1	Off Roost	Ithaca Double	20	Peters	3	6	1 1/4	1185	20	
2	Mid Morning	LC Smith	16	WA Revelation (Paper)	2 3/4	6	1 1/8	1260	20	
3	Mid Morning	Ithaca 30"	12	Winchester XX Mag	2 3/4	6	1 1/2	1260	25	
4	Mid Morning	Ithaca 30"	12	Western XX Mag	2 3/4	4	1 1/2	1260	39	killed with follow up shot
5	Mid Morning	Ithaca 30"	12	Winchester XX Mag	2 3/4	6	1 1/2	1260	30	
6	Early Morning	Ithaca 30"	12	Winchester XX Mag	2 3/4	6	1 1/2	1260	18	
7	Off Roost	Ithaca 30"	12	Winchester XX Mag	2 3/4	6	1 1/2	1260	31	flew away, fell out of air
8	Early Morning	Ithaca 30"	12	Winchester XX Mag	2 3/4	6	1 1/2	1260	45	
9	Mid Morning	Iver Johnson	12	Win. Super Speed (Paper)	2 3/4	6	1 1/4	1330	26	
10	Early Morning	Ithaca 30"	12	Fiocchi (4.5 dram)	2 3/4	6	1 3/8	1460	24	
11	Afternoon	Ithaca 30"	12	Winchester XX Mag	2 3/4	6	1 5/8	1280	25	
12	Off Roost	Mossberg	12	Federal	3 1/2	6	2 1/4	1150	35	shot legs, couldn't fly away
13	Off Roost	Mossberg	12	Federal	3 1/2	6	2 1/4	1150	44	
14	Late Morning	Mossberg	12	Winchester XX Mag	3 1/2	4	2 1/4	1150	41	
15	Mid Morning	Ithaca 30"	12	Active	2 3/4	6	1 3/4	1245	15	
16	Off Roost	LC Smith	16	Western Super X (Paper)	2 3/4	6	1 1/8	1295	15	
17	Off Roost	Ithaca 30"	12	Active	2 3/4	6	1 3/4	1245	18	
18	Off Roost	Winchester 1300	12	Winchester XX Mag	3	6	2	1175	34	
19	Afternoon	Winchester 1300	12	Winchester XX Mag	3	6	2	1175	29	
20	Late Morning	Ithaca 30"	12	Active	2 3/4	6	1 3/4	1245	19	
21	Off Roost	Winchester 1300	12	Winchester XX Mag	3	6	2	1175	35	killed with follow up shot
22	Off Roost	Ithaca 30"	12	Winchester XX Mag	2 3/4	6	1 5/8	1225	26	
23	Mid Morning	Winchester 1300	12	Winchester XX Mag	3	6	2	1175	13	
24	Afternoon	Winchester 1300	12	Winchester XX Mag	3	6	2	1175	20	
25	Off Roost	Winchester 1300	12	Winchester XX Mag	3	6	2	1175	19	
26	Noon	Ithaca 28"	12	Winchester XX Mag	2 3/4	5	1 5/8	1225	23	
27	Early Morning	Ithaca 22"	12	Active	2 3/4	6	1 3/4	1245	23	
28	Late Morning	Ithaca 28"	12	Peters	2 3/4	6	1 1/2	1260	23	
29	Late Morning	Ithaca 22"	12	Active	2 3/4	5	1 3/4	1245	29	
30	Afternoon	Ithaca New Camo	12	Winchester XX Mag	3	6	2	1175	26	
31	Mid Morning	Ithaca New Camo	12	Winchester Super XX Mag	3	6	1 7/8	1210	35	
32	Mid Morning	Ithaca New Camo	12	Winchester XX Mag	3	5	2	1175	19	
33	Early Morning	Ithaca New Camo	12	Winchester XX Mag	3	5	2	1175	20	
34	Mid Morning	Ithaca 28"	12	Active	2 3/4	6	1 3/4	1245	25	
35	Afternoon	Ithaca 16	16	Winchester XX Mag	2 3/4	6	1 1/4	1260	24	
36	Off Roost	Ithaca New Camo	12	Winchester Super XX Mag	3	6	1 7/8	1210	35	killed with follow up shot
37	Afternoon	Ithaca New Camo	12	Winchester Super XX Mag	3	6	1 7/8	1210	25	
38	Early Morning	Ithaca New Camo	12	Winchester Super XX Mag	3	6	1 7/8	1210	22	
39	Off Roost	Ithaca New Camo	12	Winchester Supreme	3	6	1 3/4	1245	15	killed with follow up shot
40	Mid Morning	Ithaca 30"	12	Winchester XX Mag	2 3/4	6	1 5/8	1225	32	
41	Off Roost	Ithaca 28"	12	Active	2 3/4	6	1 3/4	1245	21	
42	Mid Morning	Fox Sterlingworth	12	Winchester Super X	2 3/4	5	1 1/2	1260	21	
43	Early Morning	Ithaca 30"	12	Active	2 3/4	6	1 3/4	1245	22	
44	Off Roost	Fox Sterlingworth	12	Winchester Super X	2 3/4	5	1 1/2	1260	15	
45	Mid Morning	Ithaca 28"	12	Winchester XX Mag	2 3/4	6	1 5/8	1225	30	
46	Late Morning	Ithaca 28"	12	Winchester XX Mag	2 3/4	5	1 5/8	1225	29	
47	Off Roost	Ithaca 30"	12	Winchester XX Mag	2 3/4	6	1 5/8	1225	25	
48	Mid Morning	Fox Sterlingworth	12	Winchester Super X	2 3/4	6	1 1/2	1260	33	
49	Mid Morning	Ithaca 16	16	Winchester XX Mag	2 3/4	6	1 1/4	1260	27	
50	Off Roost	Ithaca 30"	12	Winchester XX Mag	2 3/4	6	1 5/8	1225	29	
51	Mid Morning	Ithaca 28"	12	Winchester XX Mag	2 3/4	5	1 5/8	1225	32	
52	Early Morning	Ithaca 28"	12	Peters	2 3/4	6	1 1/2	1260	34	
53	Mid Morning	Ithaca 28"	12	Winchester XX Mag	2 3/4	6	1 5/8	1225	26	

#	Time	Gun	Ga	Shell	Length	Shot	Load	Vel	Dist	Notes
54	Early Morning	Fox Sterlingworth	12	Peters (Paper)	2 3/4	4	1 1/4	1330	25	
55	Early Morning	Ithaca 28"	12	Winchester XX Mag	2 3/4	5	1 5/8	1225	25	
56	Early Morning	Fox Sterlingworth	12	Peters (Paper)	2 3/4	4	1 1/4	1330	28	
57	Off Roost	Ithaca 28"	12	Winchester XX Mag	2 3/4	6	1 5/8	1225	17	
58	Mid Morning	Ithaca 28"	12	Winchester Supreme	2 3/4	6	1 1/2	1260	34	
59	Early Morning	Ithaca 28"	12	Active	2 3/4	6	1 3/4	1245	26	
60	Early Morning	Ithaca 30"	12	Active	2 3/4	6	1 3/4	1245	20	
61	Off Roost	Ithaca 28"	12	Winchester XX Mag	2 3/4	5	1 5/8	1225	18	
62	Early Morning	Fox Sterlingworth	12	Win. Super Speed (Paper)	2 3/4	6	1 1/4	1330	25	
63	Mid Morning	LC Smith	16	WA Revelation (Paper)	2 3/4	6	1 1/8	1260	25	
64	Late Morning	Ithaca 30"	12	Winchester XX Mag	2 3/4	6	1 5/8	1225	24	
65	Late Morning	Fox Sterlingworth	12	Remington/Peters	2 3/4	6	1 1/2	1260	21	
66	Early Morning	Ithaca 16	16	Winchester XX Mag	2 3/4	6	1 1/4	1260	18	
67	Off Roost	Ithaca 28"	12	Active	2 3/4	5	1 3/4	1245	13	
68	Early Morning	Ithaca 28"	12	Peters	2 3/4	6	1 1/2	1260	28	
69	Early Morning	Ithaca 28"	12	Active	2 3/4	5	1 3/4	1245	31	
70	Mid Morning	Ithaca 28"	12	Active	2 3/4	5	1 3/4	1245	27	
71	Early Morning	LC Smith	16	Western SuperX Mag	2 3/4	6	1 1/4	1260	32	
72	Noon	Ithaca 16	16	Winchester XX Mag	2 3/4	6	1 1/4	1260	26	
73	Early Morning	LC Smith	16	Western SuperX Mag	2 3/4	6	1 1/4	1260	16	
74	Mid Morning	Ithaca 30"	12	Nitro Hevi-Shot	2 3/4	7.5	1 5/8	1200	30	
75	Mid Morning	Ithaca 30"	12	Peters (Paper)	2 3/4	4	1 1/4	1330	20	
76	Mid Morning	Ithaca New Water	12	Nitro Hevi-Shot	2 3/4	7.5	1 5/8	1200	20	killed with follow up shot
77	Off Roost	Ithaca New Water	12	Nitro Hevi-Shot	2 3/4	7.5	1 5/8	1200	25	killed with follow up shot
78	Early Morning	Ithaca 30"	12	Active	2 3/4	5	1 3/4	1245	20	
79	Early Morning	Fox Sterlingworth	12	Peters	2 3/4	6	1 1/2	1260	20	
80	Off Roost	Ithaca 30"	12	Winchester Super X	2 3/4	6	1 1/2	1260	25	
81	Late Morning	Ithaca 28"	12	Winchester Super X	2 3/4	6	1 1/2	1260	29	
82	Mid Morning	Ithaca 16	16	Peters	2 3/4	7.5	1 1/8	1295	14	
83	Early Morning	Ithaca 28"	12	Winchester Super X	2 3/4	6	1 1/2	1260	20	
84	Mid Morning	Ithaca 28"	12	Winchester Super X	2 3/4	6	1 1/2	1260	13	
85	Late Morning	Ithaca 30"	12	Winchester Super X	2 3/4	6	1 1/2	1260	35	killed with follow up shot
86	Early Morning	Ithaca 28"	12	Winchester XX Mag	2 3/4	6	1 5/8	1225	15	
87	Late Morning	Ithaca 30"	12	Peters	2 3/4	6	1 1/2	1260	26	
88	Off Roost	Ithaca New Water	12	Federal TSS	3	9	1 3/4	1200	18	
89	Off Roost	Ithaca 30"	12	Winchester XX Mag	2 3/4	6	1 5/8	1225	30	
90	Early Morning	Ithaca 16	16	Apex TSS	2 3/4	9	1 5/8	1150	34	
Miss 01	Off Roost	Ithaca 30"	12	Winchester XX Mag	2 3/4	6	1 1/2	1260	50	aimed off on purpose
Miss 02	Mid Morning	Mossberg	12	Federal	3 1/2	6	2 1/4	1150	20	
Miss 03	Early Morning	Mossberg	12	Federal	3 1/2	6	2 1/4	1150	35	
Miss 04	Mid Morning	Ithaca 16	16	Winchester XX Mag	2 3/4	6	1 1/4	1260	20	potluck shot
Miss 05	Mid Morning	Ithaca New Camo	12	Winchester Supreme	3	6	1 3/4	1245	20	
Miss 06	Off Roost	Ithaca 28"	12	Winchester XX Mag	2 3/4	5	1 5/8	1225	35	
Miss 07	Off Roost	Ithaca 28"	12	Active	2 3/4	6	1 3/4	1245	37	
Miss 08	Off Roost	Ithaca New Camo	12	Winchester	3	6	1 7/8	1210	15	
Miss 09	Early Morning	Fox Sterlingworth	12	Peters (Paper)	2 3/4	4	1 1/4	1330	45	
Miss 10	Mid Morning	Ithaca 28"	12	Nitro Hevi-Shot	2 3/4	7.5	1 5/8	1200	30	
Miss 11	Off Roost	Ithaca 28"	12	Winchester XX Mag	2 3/4	6	1 5/8	1225	40	twisted impossible shot
Miss 12	Early Morning	Ithaca 30"	12	Winchester	2 3/4	6	1 5/8	1225	25	potluck shot
Miss 13	Mid Morning	Ithaca 28"	12	Winchester XX Mag	2 3/4	6	1 5/8	1225	20	
Miss 14	Off Roost	Fox Sterlingworth	12	Peters (Paper)	2 3/4	4	1 1/4	1330	35	mod choke, bad pattern

THE APPRENTICE

This first set of stories begins with my first turkey killed when I was 12 and concludes with my eighth at age 18, the first turkey I legitimately called and killed on my own. My days as an apprentice were under the wing of my best friend and hunting companion, my father, and started long before I shot my first turkey. Our close relationship was unusual for father and son, held tight though our shared passion for hunting turkeys. I must have been born with a turkey-hunting gene, because I liked it from the get-go, even when I was too young to carry a gun and considering all the hard work involved in finding turkeys.

Dad had started hunting turkeys in the early 1960s, back when the sport wasn't so popular. He mostly hunted the Talladega National Forest near Brent and Centreville and was so dedicated that he drove roughly one hour and 30 minutes every day, regardless of the weather, to get to his location. Most weekdays, he'd do this and be back at work by 9 o'clock, which if you do the calculation, didn't give him much time to hunt considering the one-and-a-half-hour drive back. Despite his dedication, success was elusive. He's told me, though I wonder how much embellishment permeates the story, that he didn't hear his first turkey gobble for five years, and didn't kill his first for 13 – and all that while going every day. Of course, the season was a little shorter back then.

Dad started taking me along with him when I was four. I mostly remember walking a lot, finding and stamping out turkey tracks, and working very few turkeys. We stamped out all the turkey tracks we found because being on public lands, we didn't want others to find what we had located with great effort. Despite spending most weekends with him in the woods, I didn't see him kill a turkey until I was around 10 or so, and that was on some new private land we had gained permission to hunt. In fact, I think I only saw him kill two turkeys before I killed my first at age 12. Turkey hunting was just different back then without the populations and understanding of turkey behavior we have today. Our calling was more subdued, and you had to walk a lot to find a gobbling turkey.

This span of stories is notable for a change in hunting habitat that starts in mixed timber hills then changes with the discovery of a bottomland tract along the Black Warrior River. My first kills took place on several smaller private tracts in Coosa County (Taliaferro Farm, Rolling Place and LBV Farm), a large tract of mountainous hardwoods nearby (Clay County), and a large tract of upland woods with pasture in Chilton County (Betty Jeane's Farm). While Betty Jeane's had some pasture, we mostly hunted turkeys in woods, including the national forest where I never did kill a turkey.

I learned all my basics from Dad in these early years including the minimal calling technique and walking great distances in search of gobbling turkeys. I was his apprentice and we were, strangely perhaps, best of friends. I followed all his leads — where to listen, trailing him in our approach to a gobbling turkey, and letting him pick out my tree. By the end of these apprentice years, I was challenging his decisions and eager to go it alone, though I'd come to find that his companionship remained integral and necessary to my hunting enjoyment, and our close relationship continues to this day.

Our eventual introduction to a phenomenal bottomland tract in Hale County on the Black Warrior River (Swampy Acres) offered a turkey hunting experience that seemed altogether different from that in the hills where we'd always hunted. First, it held unfathomable numbers of turkeys with multiples often heard gobbling from a single location at the crack of dawn. Second, there were no hills to maneuver around and make an approach. By and large, if a turkey could be heard, you couldn't get very close, especially early in the season before the leaves were out. It was in this bottomland tract where I legitimately called and killed my first turkey on my own. After shooting him, I was so excited to share the experience with Dad, since he wasn't with me, that I left the turkey lying right where I shot him, went and found Dad hunting on the other side of the property, and brought him back to show and detail the events to him directly. Finding him and coming back to the location took an hour or so, which thinking back now, I realize how stupid that was to leave that turkey lying there on the forest floor unguarded. What if a predator had found and run off with him? I'd have been devastated. But he was still there and I got to detail the whole operation to Dad, who was filled paternal pride.

Kill 1 Spring 1985 – Coosa County (Rolling Place)

*Spring '85
* FIRST
    Turkey
* Jake
* Rolling Place
Coosa County

Bob
Jr.

Kill 2 March 29, 1986 – Coosa County (Taliaferro Farm)

*March 29, 1986
*18 pounds

*9 inch beard
*L.C: Smith
*9:45 AM
Coosa County: The Farm

Highlights

* Dad was asleep
  when Bob Jr.
  called and shot
  gobbler

* didn't gobble

* 2nd turkey

Bob Jr.

L-A199

Kill 3 March 19, 1988 – Coosa County (LBV Farm)

March 19, 1988 – Opening Day
weight – 21¼ LB.
spurs – 1 inch
beard 9½ inches
time – 2:08 PM
Black – Lanny Vines
3rd Turkey

Summary

It was a cold and windy day.
we went to the farm and hunted
till 10:00. we had heard nothing
or seen nothing. we went back
to the house and took a nap.
we went to take a ham to
Willy (Lanny Vines property care taker)
we drove around and got out
to walk a road. I took a gun
& dad didn't. we spooked a gobbler
and circled around to about
where he was. Dad called and saw
me raise my gun. I had heard him
drum and walk. He stepped out
and I ... what do you think I did

Kill 4 April 3, 1988 – Chilton County (Betty Jeane's Farm)

Easter Sunday – Dad and I sat by the field after we had hunted that morning. Dad laid down to sleep and later I did too. In a little while, Dad woke me up very quietly because he saw hens in the field. We watched them feed on the other side for 15 minutes. I got tired so I laid my gun down. In a minute, I heard walking on the path next to us. A gobbler walked down the path and saw the hens feeding. He started walking fast to them. He got in the field, still walking to them, and I waited until a bush was between us. I raised my gun. Still walking, he got to an open area between us. I clucked and he stopped to look for me. Dad said to shoot him, but a small pine tree was between us. He looked too far, but I shot. I knocked him down, he got up, then flew 10 feet and fell down again. He got back up and was flying across the field. Dad took him in the air.

Kill 5 March 30, 1990 – Chilton County (Betty Jeane's Farm)

It was raining when we arrived in the morning. We stayed in Dad's truck and slept until 7:30. It still raining, we walked around trying to find turkeys in the fields. I spotted about eight turkeys past the peninsula and they appeared to be gobblers. Dad and I went around to where they were headed and set up. We felt this setup was bad, so we walked the back road a little further. Dad suddenly saw them very close in the field. We immediately squatted and found two bad trees. They were so bad that we then crawled up to a good pine tree in front of us. We could see the turkeys very well. There appeared to be three gobblers, two of which were strutting, and three hens. Dad yelped and the two gobbled back. After a long time, the hens made their way into the woods where we were. One of the hens had a beard and at first we thought it was a jake. The gobblers followed into the woods slowly. They made their way into range. While waiting for a shot on one of the two in front of us, the third came up to our left. I had a shot and counted to three so that Dad and I could shoot one at the same time. Dad had his gun on the one to the left and easy shot. On three, I shot but Dad didn't. He wanted to watch me. I had taken my first Oakmulgee turkey.

Kill 6 April 30, 1990 – Hale County (Swampy Acres)

Dad and I had permission to hunt Swampy Acres that Friday until Monday. Dad killed a giant Saturday and a jake Sunday. I was down in the dumps, because this place was awesome and I hadn't killed one (yet). Monday morning, we arrived early in the woods and set up on the edge of a field where Dad had killed his two the previous days. We heard and saw nothing. Finally, we decided to leave but before we did, we checked another field. When we drove in the field, we saw a lot of turkeys run out of the field into the woods (Lynn's Bottom). We eased off into the woods and walked closer to where they might be. We sat at two bad trees. We yelped and one gobbled in front of us about 150 yards. We changed to better trees. This took a minute so I picked my tree and sat down because I was afraid he might be coming. Dad was in front of me telling me to get closer but I wouldn't. Finally, Dad yelped to see if the turkey would gobble, and we would know if we could get closer. The turkey gobbled about 50 yards in front of us. Dad didn't know what to do because he wasn't sitting against a tree, and he was between me and the turkey. Dad decided to lay back on the ground and cover his ears. I thought the turkey would come right over him. In about 30 seconds, I saw a gobbler walking fast towards me and a little towards my right. Next, he disappeared behind some brush and reappeared on the other side very close. He was walking straight towards me. He got closer and stuck his head up real quick, but still sort of walking. There were some leaves in my shooting path, but he was so close – I shot. I ran up and he was graveyard dead. Dad was so surprised to see how quick it had happed, and that it had happened. He was a beautiful turkey.

Kill 7   December, 1990 – Clay County

December, 1990
Time - 6:30 A.M.
Place - Clay County (The Ridge)
A Juke / 31 steps
7th turkey

Summary

Dad and I seperated
early in the morning
about 60 yards apart on
top of the big ridge. I
immediatley heard yelping.
I was slightly on the left
side of the ridge and I
heard walking on the
other side. I yelped
awesome. After 5 minuets,

the walking went
away. Then I heard
a juke yelp. I yelped
back. He showed him
self immediatly. He was
looking at me. He looked
too far, but I shot (low).
I knew he wasn't dead.
He started running and
I tried to chase him.
I stopped to listen where
he was running. I saw
him flying high up in
the air and then he
just fell. I ran down
and found him dead
on the ground.

[I included this kill as a miss in the data section which is debatable. He did die from the shot, but he flew pretty far before dying midair. Effective turkey shots leave them flopping in their tracks.]

Kill 8   March 23, 1991 – Hale County (Swampy Acres)

Having gone to Swampy Acres the year before and knowing that spring break would be during turkey season, Dad and I made plans to go to Swampy Acres for a whole week of nonstop hunting. We were excited and almost positive that we would get one, being that the year before we came for three days and went home with three turkeys. The first morning we decided to hunt different areas, and I was pumped about going by myself. We woke up at 4:32 and dressed. I took the Jeep and headed to Lynn's Bottom. As soon as I got out, clouds came rolling over and wind started blowing. I headed to my listening spot. As the wind blew, I knew they wouldn't gobble so I decided to go ahead and set up where I had seen 28 turkeys a couple months before during a scouting exploration.

Daylight came slowly and I yelped softly every 15 minutes. Around 6:15, the wind started to die down. I thought I heard a faint gobble to my left and across the field, but I wasn't sure. At 6:30, just as I got up to move, I thought I heard another gobble in the same direction as before. I eased across the side of the field and set up in a clump of big trees that broke my outline and hid me well. I made a few soft yelps and clucks with Dad's old Lynch box. They sounded so good that I almost wanted to gobble myself. Shortly after, I started to hear some clucking about 75 yards in front of me. I got ready, but it soon stopped.

About five more minutes went by when I saw movement about 60 yards away and slightly to my left. My eyes caught the meanest damn turkey you've ever seen. His head was bright white, a little blue, and blood red at the bottom. I could see his beard swinging. He was headed right and I lost him in a bunch of thick stuff straight out in front of me. I suspected he would come up on the right side. He reappeared about 55 yards away, walking slowly towards me. He stopped at 45 yards, put his head back, pulled his feathers up, and drummed. He came out of his strut and brushed his head against his body to get the mosquitoes off. He did this back and forth for about 10 minutes. He was too far for me to shoot though just barely, so I sat as still as I have ever been. I could see him well. I was dying but knew if I waited, he would come a little closer. Slowly, he began to peck things on the ground and started to feed on off. He was leaving, and I was helplessly mad. He got behind a tree and I gave a soft cluck or two. He turned around, strutted, and took a few steps back to me, but that's all. In another few minutes, I started losing him again. When he got behind a tree, I gave a soft yelp. Again, he stopped, turned around, and strutted. I told myself if he ever got back to where he had been earlier, I was going to take a long shot. He started walking closer and a little more to the right. Finally, he got back to the same distance. I was ready. He stepped out into a perfect alley for my shot to take him. He took three steps closer and stood up. He was far, but the hell if I was going to leave him in the woods. I superimposed the bead on his wattles and squeezed my right forefinger. With pride, after my first successful alone hunt without Dad, I walked out of the woods with 22 pounds slung over my shoulder.

TAKING FLIGHT

After turning 18 and killing a turkey on my own, I set off to college in Tuscaloosa and started hunting almost as much as I wanted. Though I was out of the house and on my own, Dad and I kept our close bond and still hunted together often. Either I'd go home to hunt with him on the weekends or he'd come to hunt the locations I'd found close to school before going back to work on the weekdays. Though we didn't have unfettered access to Swampy Acres, we were still permitted several trips there each season, and it was close to Tuscaloosa. Over the next several years, we killed many turkeys there. And while having access to such prime turkey habitat afforded us much success, one change in tactic really transformed my turkey hunting for the better – I began calling louder and more aggressively. I learned to do this from watching Will Primos' very first video on turkey hunting titled "The Truth." In it, he and Cuz Strickland discussed their loud and aggressive calling and how effective it was. I was so in awe of their calling, and the awesome gobbling they got on film, that I made an audio recording of their video and played it over and over in my vehicle. I started using a Primos True Double then and still do, though I probably call less aggressively now, perhaps because turkeys gobble less these days.

A couple years into college, we joined a large hunting club in Pickens County in west Alabama, Triple C, but continued hunting our traditional areas on the other side of the state too – the private tracts in Coosa County (Taliaferro Farm, Rolling Place, and LBV Farm) and Clay County. As good as Swampy Acres was, Triple C was at least as good if not better. It was more traditional upland woods managed with pine plantations, loaded with turkeys, and had little competition. We killed a lot of turkeys there. I also hunted the Oakmulgee Wildlife Management area of the national forest, and while it was vast and remote, and I found some gobbling turkeys from time to time, it was difficult and unproductive. Swampy Acres and Triple C made us look like good turkey hunters.

You'd think at this stage in my life, a college kid out of the house, that I'd leave the relationship with my father behind to pursue the world without him. But our bond only deepened. When hunting together we became a single unit, thinking and moving in rhythm. Our deep friendship, forged upon a mutual respect for one another and a deep love for hunting wild turkeys in the pristine outdoors, helped keep my head focused at school and out of trouble. I had always wanted to go to medical school, and this friendship and love for turkey hunting outcompeted typical college activities that could have derailed such aspirations. Those were really good times.

We also continued to fall hunt the mountainous Clay County property which we had done for many years. Aside from the joys of working the deep hardwoods in search of droves, fall hunting was mostly unproductive as I only killed a few turkeys. Our love for fall hunting eventually waned, giving way to a passion for duck hunting. I haven't gone on a fall turkey hunt in 25 years.

In this next group of stories, you'll also see the beginnings of another theme to mark my hunting career – the passion for using different weapons for killing turkeys, especially nostalgic ones. Dad had long hunted with an old Ithaca Model 37 pump 12-gauge; in fact he had two or three of them, and an L.C. Smith 16-gauge double barrel. I killed my second turkey with the L.C. back when it wasn't so old and nostalgic. But in the 1990s, the advent of 3 ½-inch magnums spurred an onslaught of modern guns. I got a Mossberg 835 Ulti-Mag chambered for 3 ½-inch shells, but after missing a few and destroying my shoulder, traded it in for a new Winchester pump chambered for 3-inch shells. I ended up not liking it either and eventually went back to our tried-and-true Ithaca pumps chambered for 2 ¾-inch shells with the occasional use of the L.C. Smith. Since we still hunted on the move by finding and chasing gobbling turkeys, carrying a light gun became more important to me than maximizing firepower. The Ithaca Gun Company came back into business in the late 1990s and started producing the Model 37 again, this time chambered for 3-inch shells. So we bought a couple. We also found an old 16-gauge Model 37 at a gun show and bought it too. All in all, we've always carried a variety of guns, finding joy in shooting turkeys with different guns throughout a season.

Kill 9 November 30, 1991 – Clay County

It was my first year at college, and I was very eager to get home for the Thanksgiving holidays. Dad and I were greatly looking forward to going hunting. As usual, we went to Clay County Thanksgiving morning. We saw and heard nothing. When we were driving out, we rounded a slight turn and saw two big, black turkeys fly off. Then another followed, and another, and two more. We counted 10 and decided to go after them a couple days later.

Saturday came around and Dad and I headed back. We stopped by the house, and Mark signed us out for the area below the ridge. He had seen a lot of scratching down in there. Dad and I slipped into the woods while it was still dark and found two good trees. Morning came, and we called, but didn't see anything. After 30 minutes, we walked the area trying to find the elusive birds. We heard and saw nothing. Finally, we decided to hit the farm. Driving out of their property in my new Chevy Blazer, I wanted to stop and hunt behind Willy Wilson's ridge for about an hour. We got out, grabbed our stuff, and walked the mile (it seemed like) up the mountain.

At the top, we stopped and listened for scratching – nothing. Dad didn't seem too into hunting the place since it was so hilly, but I just had to work the hollows. Finally, we started working down the mountain, listening every 100 yards.

I guess I am going to have to admit something: Dad and I had borrowed Billy's Bionic Ear and were using it to listen for scratching. Here we were in these beautiful woods, away from technology with headphones on and holding a big sound dish. Tom Kelly would have been disappointed. But anyway, we got pretty far down and worked off on a side ridge. It was so beautiful and turkey looking that we decided to sit down for a few minutes. I picked a great tree, sat down, put my head net on, and started scratching in the leaves with a stick and purring like turkeys do when they feed. It sounded good. I did this for about 15 minutes.

Eventually, I heard a soft yelp down the hollow to my left, and I answered. The turkey yelped again, and it sounded like a hen. The turkey yelped a few more times, each time was closer. My heart was pounding. I was in position. One yelp sounded like it might have been a gobbler. Finally, I started hearing walking and a hen came up in front of me about 25 yards. She stopped and yelped. Then I heard more walking behind her. Another hen came up and then three jakes. The turkeys stopped and were looking for me. The woods were awesome, I had an old Iver Johnson single shot in my hands with an old paper shell, and the jakes were standing tall

– I couldn't stand it. I cocked the hammer, put the bead on one of their necks and squeezed the trigger to let the hammer slam down. Boy, was it sweet.

After shooting, we decided to try and call them back to see if Dad could kill one with his old Newport single shot. We waited 30 minutes, sat at the same trees, and started calling. One answered to the right. We called back and forth but she wouldn't come very far. Finally, Dad saw two walking away about 100 yards out. I called again and we heard running to our left. A jake came running up and stopped about 25 yards. Dad let his Newport single shot sound off, and we each had a bird. We walked out of the woods side-by-side with two jakes over our shoulders. Their wings were a picture-perfect flopping. Tom Kelly would have been proud after all.

Kill 10 April 15, 1992 – Hale County (Swampy Acres)

Spring season came and I was ready to hunt. In college now and somewhat out on my own, I've never been more fired up about a season than this one. I went scouting a few times before season began to find places to hunt near Tuscaloosa. Buck Burns, a legendary turkey hunter, showed me some areas too, mainly in the national forest. Well, season came and I hunted almost every day. It was a late season, and I didn't hear a gobble for two weeks.

Finally, the gobbling cranked up. One day in the management area, I called up a hot turkey, but he saw me before I saw him and took off. It was getting late in the season, but it seemed the hunting was just now getting good. Dad called me on Tuesday and said that we were going to hunt Swampy Acres in the morning. After spending the night in the cabin and talking to James, who is the smartest person I've ever met (and most annoying – he won't ever stop talking), we got up to a somewhat overcast but still morning. Dad took the four-wheeler and went to Lynn Bottom and Gin House Ponds. I took the truck and went behind Touson. I drove to the top of the big field, parked and walked to the bottom to listen, which wasn't easy considering I had one broken toe with a bad laceration on it [that's another story]. I was slow. Finally, I got to the listen spot. It was dark. At five till six, I owled and one gobbled straight in the woods and a long ways off. For 10 minutes, I couldn't make him gobble again. I finally eased in the woods and set up on a tree. The place was beautiful. The leaves were partially out and the ground was solid green from a carpet of weeds. Also, two-foot-tall weeds with big yellow tops were everywhere.

I thought how awesome it would be to kill one there. I slipped in my True Double, got out my push button and slate, and began to tree call. He immediately gobbled to my left and not far. Since I couldn't spin on my tree, I found another close by. I probably could have gotten closer, but I decided to just call him from there. I called softly and he was hot. After five minutes, I cackled and then poured it to him just like Primos would do in his videos. I got him so hot – he started gobbling like crazy. After 20 minutes, he stopped for a while and I was ready. Fifteen minutes went by – nothing. Suddenly, way behind me and to my left, I thought I heard a gobble though I wasn't sure. After another minute, I heard it again. I knew he was far but I also knew bottomlands made turkeys seem farther than they really are. I got up and moved 50 yards towards him, found a good tree and called. He responded, and then his next gobble sounded closer and moving to my left. I could see a long way through the woods to the field. I saw something walk by real far. It was running to my right.

After five minutes, he gobbled 50 yards away and 90 degrees to my right. I got ready left handed. I called softly and he gobbled. It was so cool. His gobble was one that echoed. He wanted everyone in the county to hear him. I sure did. The next time he gobbled he sounded just a bit farther, so I spun and aimed towards him. One minute elapsed. I called softly and he responded. After another minute of silence, he gobbled 30 yards away and a little to my left. I immediately saw him walking towards me. I could see his red head, but he looked small. He went behind a big tree, I got my gun up, he came out into an opening, and my bead was on his neck. Any time you shoot a gun, there is a point where you are committed to pulling the trigger and nothing can stop you – even though you haven't shot yet. At this point for me, just when I was about to pull the trigger, I saw a turkey gobble just to the left of the one I was pulling the trigger on. I shot, turkeys flew away, and I ran up to find I had killed a jake. I was very disappointed. I shot the wrong bird. But it was still fun. On my behalf, I would like to say that the jake was very mature looking. I guess I'll have to kill that mature one another time. Till then, I hope he lives well.

Kill 11 March 24, 1993 – Hale County (Swampy Acres)

March 20 rolled around and it was time to hit the woods again. Nothing happened the first two days of season in the management area, so my desire to hear one gobble only increased. After two rainy days, a beautiful Wednesday rolled around and I couldn't stand it. I decided to go to the Chandler Place after my thermodynamics course at 1 p.m. I got there about 2:30, changed in the car, pumped the old 30-inch Ithaca and hit the field.

It wasn't five minutes before I spotted 13 turkeys across the big field – and they looked like gobblers. How was I going to get to them? I spent the next 45 minutes walking way around the field so I could cut across to the other side without spooking them. I set up on the edge of the woods fairly close to where I thought they would be. After 20 minutes of calling and hearing nothing, I decided to sneak closer. I was cutting through a finger woods thinking they were on the other side. Finally, I saw them. But I still had to get closer. It was risky, but I did. I got close enough to see the field well and saw turkeys running away. Some then stopped and were standing tall, looking at me. I could see red on their heads. Though it appeared I had spooked them, I called to see what would happen. I yelped and two gobbled back. I yelped again, and they responded again. Then I saw the turkeys turn and start running towards me. They got closer; I called again, and they gobbled but seemingly farther away than the turkeys that were running towards me. Five turkeys came into the woods and in range. I knew they were gobblers, but didn't know if they were jakes. Finally, one stuck his bright blue head up – I took him at 25 steps. He was a jake. Dang.

Miss 1 March 25, 1993 – Hale County (Swampy Acres)

It was 4:15 in the morning, and I was going to try and get one of the big boys I had heard gobble the previous afternoon. I knew where they would be, because the day before, I called up five jakes and two gobbling big boys which were behind them still out in the field. I killed one of the jakes, and now I wanted a mature bird. I was listening at 4:45 on the edge of the field where I shot my jake the day before. I heard one gobble early to my right, on that huge swamp that runs from Swain all the way down the side of the Chandler Place. I didn't hear anything again for 10 more minutes. I then decided to sit up on the edge of the finger of woods facing that swap. It was a long way across the field to where I thought he was, and there was cotton in the field. I started tree calling, and he started gobbling. He was straight across from me. I started multi-hen calling and cutting, and he started gobbling like crazy. The hens started yelping everywhere. A couple were behind me and a few over with him. Every time I yelped or a hen did, he gobbled. This went on for 10 minutes. Then everything got silent.

I thought that there was no way he would be coming across the field, through cotton, and away from hens to me. But in three minutes, he gobbled in the cotton a lot closer. I gave one small yelp. Ahead of me was what looked like 30 yards of open space and then cotton. I knew if he was coming through the cotton, I would hear him. I was ready. Three more minutes passed. Finally, I heard something. Then I saw his fan coming towards me. The fan went down and this bright blue head came up. I was so nervous. The turkey kept coming, slowly. He finally made it close to the edge of the cotton and stuck his head up. Then he stood up real tall like he saw me. I knew this was it – booooommmm. I jumped up and two were flying away already 60 yards out there. One of them was mine. I tried to pump my gun, but it was jammed. I looked around to make sure one wasn't flopping on the ground. There was nothing. I had missed – completely. It didn't even knock him down. I remember aiming high because I thought the gun shot low. After future patterning, the gun shot straight as an arrow. It was my first turkey to miss, and I was sick – little did I know about the rest of the season ahead.

[This was an unusual example of patterning a gun that ended up costing me this turkey. During the season, I patterned the gun one windy day finding that it shot low and off to one side leading me to think the gun's aim was way off. So I shot this turkey by aiming high and a little to the other side to compensate. As recorded, this ended in failure. A follow up patterning on a non-windy day found the gun shot perfectly straight. I believe the wind messed up my pattern that first day leading me to aim off.]

Kill 12 March 28, 1993 – Hale County (Swampy Acres)

Spring season came around – it was time for Dad and me to take our annual Spring Break week off for solid turkey hunting. We were excited because we had Swampy Acres for the first half of the week. The first day there started as usual – Dad killed one early behind Touson that gobbled his head off. I was at Swain and heard it all, which was a lot of fun. The rest of the day was dry, but that evening I roosted one in Lynn's Bottom. He gobbled three times after he flew up. I felt real good about the next morning. Dad and I were going to go together so Dad could try filming a hunt. We went to sleep that night not knowing which side of the swamp to get on. I thought he was on the Gray field side, but the Lynn Bottom side had more woods.

Morning came in and we decided to listen at the shooting house near Lynn's Bottom. It wasn't two minutes before a loud gobble broke the silence. We quickly walked down the field. He gobbled again, and we smiled. We eased across the bottom of the field and into the wooded area we wanted to set up in. By now, he had gobbled two more times roosted over the swamp.

He was far out over it – perhaps the other side would've been better. We found two big trees, set up and hoped to call him our direction. Dad was to my right where he could film good. It was real dark, so I started my soft multi-call yelping. I used my Primos box, True Double, push-button, and slate. Boy, did that get him gobbling. After a few minutes of this, I heard flying and saw the silhouette of a big bird against the early morning light coming toward us. It lit high on a big limb over the edge of the swap, 70 yards in front us. The big bird turned sideways so I could see the silhouette of a beard hanging down from his huge belly. It was real neat watching him on the limb. It was still pretty dark, so I knew he probably wouldn't see me, but I didn't want to call and have him look right at me either.

To my right, I heard Dad narrating for the video and clearing his throat. I wanted to strangle him – what if he spooked the turkey away. I later learned he hadn't seen the turkey fly over and didn't know he was right there in front of us. The gobbler paid no attention to Dad's noise – I was relieved. The turkey stayed in the tree for five minutes. A couple times, he turned away and I gave a light yelp. I was afraid if he didn't see a hen over by us, he would fly back to where he had been. Finally, he turned, spread his wings and took to flight. But he went straight down.

My heart was pounding – I felt confident. I gave a light yelp as he was out of sight, down by the swamp. After a couple minutes, I saw his glowing blue head cutting through the dark and easing to my left. He was out of range. Twice he stopped to strut his action. Little did he know that the Mossberg was waiting on him. He got far enough to my left that I had to take the gun off my knee. I was worried because the Mossberg was heavy, and I didn't know how long I would have to hold it.

Then he turned and headed my way. I got ready as he moved into range. He stopped and stuck his head up. I had a shot, but wanted him closer. Then he started moving towards me again. He looked so good as he was getting close. He got to a good clean area, Dad yelped, causing him to stand up tall looking. I put the bead on his neck and pulled the trigger. I got him, but somehow had only shot his legs. He wasn't able to stand and take flight before I got on him. Dad got it all on film. It's always great killing one with Dad.

[This was about the time that camcorders hit the market. A friend had given Dad one which we used to film many turkey hunts over the next several years. Dad was more often the filmer as I was perhaps more eager to pull the trigger. Also, this kill was included as one of the misses in the data section. While I killed him with one shot, I had only shot and broken his legs. I think he wasn't able to run and take flight to get away. It was also my first use of the new Mossberg 3 ½-inch chambered gun. I'm not sure why I shot so low as it was a fairly easy shot. Perhaps it was too heavy for me.]

Miss 2 April 2, 1993 – Taliaferro Farm

Dad and I slipped across the top field around mid-morning. We sat at two different trees. After an hour, I cutted – one gobbled across the field. He worked into the field and gobbled and drummed. Finally, he worked into the woods. Too thick to shoot through– he was real close when I saw his eye peering through a small hole in the brush– he putted and walked away. Dad and I both then took a poor shot at the same time and both missed. He flew away. Don't think we wounded him. Would have been an awesome one. I blamed him seeing us all on the camouflage.

Kill 13 April 23, 1993 – Hale County (Swampy Acres)

It was close to the end of season, and we wanted to try our luck at Swampy Acres again. I met Dad Thursday afternoon at Paul's Sporting Goods, and we went together to afternoon hunt. We saw two turkeys in Lynn Bottom and many tracks around the area. I knew where I would be in the morning.

Morning came, and we headed out. The fields were foggy. We got out into the nippy air and finished gathering our stuff. We waited three minutes by the shooting house before one gobbled down near the lake. My blood started pumping. We hurried down the edge of the field. Halfway down, we stopped, thinking that he may be closer than we first realized. I owled twice and nothing happened. We eased into the woods and I owled again, real loud. He gobbled across the bottom of the field where I had killed one previously in the year. It was a rough gobble – he seemed young.

Easing through the woods to the edge of the field, I wanted to make him gobble again. I owled twice, but nothing. After another minute of silence and fearful we had spooked him, we finally heard him gobble just across the field. We couldn't get around the field like I wanted. We found a good tree, 15 yards off the field that was big and hidden. I took my calls and started multi-calling. Two hens in the swamp behind me and to my left started cutting, so I started cutting. The turkey gobbled once more. After a few minutes, the hens flew out into the field on the other side. I thought one was a gobbler. I could barely see them because of the fog. I proceeded to try to call them over. One of them yelped every once in a while. They started slowly feeding over to us.

In the meantime, I didn't know where the gobbler was. The hens got to us and started feeding to our right. Then across the field, a strutting dude came into view. He turned sideways and I saw a short beard – a jake. He looked good though, with a bright blue head. He slowly strutted our way. I was afraid the hens were feeding off and he would follow them. I called some more. He got halfway across the field and stopped right in front of us. He stayed there for a while. I could hear the hens yelping some. Suddenly, the hens started cutting and flew over the swap. He gobbled when they did that. I now knew he was mine. He stayed where he was for five more minutes. Finally, he walked a little closer. He was still far, so I wasn't going to shoot, but he stood up for a while and presented such a great shot, and since I had the Mossberg with 3 ½-inch magnum shell, I decided to take him home. At 44 steps, the Mossberg did a number on his head and neck. It was a lot of fun.

Miss 3 April 27, 1993 – Hale County (Swampy Acres)

It happened so perfectly; the air was still, the temperature was just nippy enough to give that fresh feeling, the sun was shining off the dew on the green carpet of grasses that covered the beautiful old forest floor around me, and the gobble of a mature tom's voice was the echo of my keen hen box making her sound in the untamed air. He came up all right, with a buddy leading the way. My hopes are that he is still out there looking for a last-of-the-season hen, but my worries are that his feathers are scattered around the edge of a swamp.

The night before, Dad and I met at Paul's so we could spend the night at Swampy Acres camp house. For some reason, I really wanted to hunt the end of Keaton Lake field in the morning. There had always been turkeys there in the past, and a few days before we had seen some tracks and even some turkeys in that area. Knowing the weather report, I knew if there was one down there, we would hear him gobble. Morning came and what an awesome morning it was. Dad and I eased down the side of Keaton. The grass was high, our legs got wet as hell. Also, the sun was rising pretty good, so I was worried that if one was roosted on the side, he would see us. We got to the bottom at 5:45 and opened our ears. Nothing for 15 minutes. It was such a beautiful morning that it was hard for me to believe we weren't hearing anything.

Dad and I decided to sit down for a few minutes and see if we could get one to gobble by calling. But five minutes of silence toyed with our patience. We wanted to go somewhere else and get one gobbling. Our plan was to ease across the creek over to Alabama field and work our way back through the Gin House area to the truck. Like usual we saw no turkeys in Alabama field. We snuck up to the Gin House field hoping to see one strutting his action out in the middle, but there was nothing. All along the road between the two fields there were lots of fresh gobbler tracks. Off to our left were the areas that we sometimes referred to as the park (of Swampy Acres). That area is so beautiful. It is old woods with a big swamp 100 yards from the field. Each year as spring brings nature to life, a dense, green carpet of grasses and weeds covers the floor of the woods. It is just simply beautiful. Dad and I had always talked about how beautiful a big gobbler would look coming through there. It was time to give a yelp.

I pulled out my trusty hen box and sounded off with the yelp – nothing. I let two more go and 100 yards away through the woods came a crisp gobble. We quickly turned our heads to look for trees. Once again, Dad had a video camera, so finding the right trees was hard. Finally, we got set up. I yelped to see where he was and he responded again. We didn't know if we should move closer, so we stayed. Two minutes passed, and I yelped again. He responded in the same place. All of a sudden I saw a mass of turkey heads, close and walking straight to me. They got to a big fallen tree and the first one hopped on it. My bead was on it, but I saw that it was a jake. He hopped down and three others followed. They were all jakes. The first one got 10 steps from me and began to lightly putt. The others joined in. They weren't very alarmed though. You know how stupid jakes are.

After a few seconds they slowly eased off. When they were out of sight, I gave another yelp. A minute later I saw the jakes coming back. One got 10 steps from me – again – and started the light putting – again. And then – once again – they slowly eased away. When they got out of sight I heard Dad whispering to me. I turned and hoped he had gotten them on film. When I saw him, he had his gun up asking if he could shoot one of those jakes. I said yes, and we tried to call them back. After we yelped a couple times, the turkey gobbled a little further off. We decided to move closer. We picked up our stuff and walked 75 yards closer. We delayed for a long time picking out two trees. Finally, we found two and got set up. I yelped. It wasn't a minute while I was still moving stuff from under my butt that I heard Dad. I looked at him and he told me he was seeing turkeys. I thought it would be the jakes, but I still got ready. Then my eyes picked up something way out in front of me. It moved a little, and I could tell it was a turkey. Then another came into view behind it. It looked like the second one had his fan spread out. Finally, I could tell it was strutting and the fan was round, not like a jake. That was him, a big boy. I wanted a mature tom so bad. The first one headed my way, and the second one followed slowly. They both got down in a little dip kind of out of sight, so I sunk lower in my sitting position to get in better shooting position. My heart started pounding. The first one came out walking at an angle to my right. He was getting close to range. I saw a tremendously, long and skinny beard, but I wanted the one behind him. As the first one casually walked by at 40 yards, the other came marching behind him. He was following the same path cut by the lead bird. He got to an area that would give me a clean, but long shot if he stopped, but he wasn't about to slow down. I gave a yelp to make him stop, but he took a few more steps. Then, just before he got behind a big tree, his motion ceased, and he threw his head up high. I put the bed of the Mossberg chambered with 3 ½-inch magnum on his wattles and boooomm. I jumped up and saw him behind some thick stuff. I saw that he had been knocked down, but now he was farther to the right of where I shot him. I took off in a sprint as I knew he wasn't hit good. Then I saw him running away. I had a good shot. I threw the Mossberg up and nailed him pretty good. My shot knocked him down and he paused on the ground for a second. Then he spread his wings and took flight. I was running fast and not far behind him. He disappeared out of sight, and that was the last I ever heard or saw him. We spent the next 30 minutes searching the area for him. Dad was real mad – I was too. The next day, we went back and tried to figure it all out. Dad had gotten some of it on tape, but he was filming that first one when I shot. We searched the area again but came up empty handed. I still have a hard time believing I missed. It was my third miss for the season. You can be sure that I'm going to correct my problem before next year.

Kill 14 March 25, 1994 – Hale County (Swampy Acres)

Once again, Dad and I had the opportunity to hunt Swampy Acres. Our hopes were high as we'd killed a lot of turkeys there over the previous few years. We slept Thursday night in the old lodge. Confidence radiated from my eyes realizing we had always killed so many turkeys. The forecast called for a bad morning with clearing early. As usual, we hit Swain early, but nothing. It was cloudy and windy. After a small breakfast, we decided to test Dad's new truck, "Greenfield," on the Gin House ponds, stopping off for a quick peek at Keaton. Once again, nothing. Coming in the back-side of Alabama, Dad urged for a quick peek in the Gin House field. I was ready to leave, so I went to get the truck while he checked. As I drove Greenfield back through the Alabama field to get Dad, he came running and motioning me to stop the truck. I thought why? If he saw one in the field, why is he so worried? I got out and he motioned me to come quickly. I had to get all my stuff out of the back.

As I eased over to Dad, he took off running. Running? I followed in a trot. But why were we running if he saw one in the field? Finally, halfway between Alabama and Gin House, he stopped. It never crossed my mind that he could have made one gobble, but he had. We searched for two trees and found them quickly which is always easy at Swampy Acres. We quickly set up and called. Nothing. Had we spooked him? The setting was beautiful with big trees and an open understory. I figured I could see for 150 yards. Dad was set up to shoot if he came straight on or to the right. I was set up to take the left.

For the next 15 minutes, Dad gave some good yelps, but nothing. Dad grew impatient. We both thought we had spooked the turkey. I made us sit for 15 more minutes. Finally, way out, I saw a black object and tail go behind a tree at 85 yards. "There he is," I told dad. After 30 seconds, he appeared again but only for a split second. Then after 30 more seconds, he appeared, put his wings down, pulled his fan up, and fluffed his feathers in an attempt to entice me over. He was enticing me all right, but I wasn't about to budge. He was moving left and coming in. Then two more long-beards appeared behind them.

Following Dad's command, I clucked to coax him in. At 70 yards, a fallen tree posed a problem for the bird as he paced back and forth try-ing to figure out how to get around it. He finally hopped on top of it and decided it was a great place to strut. His head was red, white, and blue. After a minute of displaying, he hopped off the stage and came in slowly strutting every 10 steps. The others were coming in also. Finally, I thought I might be able to take him with the 3 ½-inch magnum. He stopped, put that head up, kind of acted like something was suspicious, and I shot. My shot was bad, again, not hitting his head and neck well, but I took him to the freezer.

Kill 15 March 27, 1994 – Hale County (Swampy Acres)

Dang it, another jake. I've been haunted by jakes the past few years. I don't mean to kill them, it just happens, usually by accident. Our third day at Swampy Acres brought our third turkey while there. After early morning hunting, Dad and I walked the back road behind Swain field. We eased our way along, yelping and sitting every now and then. About halfway down, Dad thought he heard a cluck. We sat down by the road; I was in front of Dad. Dad threw out some sweet notes with his jake yelper – hobble hobble hobble down the road and close. After a couple of minutes, Dad yelped again – hobble hobble hobble. He sounded good. We waited for him to come up the road. Three turkeys showed up about 40 yards down. I could barely see as one of them went into a strut. Dad and I both believe it was a mature fan; hobble hobble hobble again. They eventually came on up the road closer. I had pinpointed the one that strutted and gobbled (I thought). I followed his head until he was 15 steps. Since my bead was on his wattles the entire time, I never saw his beard. The shot was there. I even questioned if it could be a jake, but his head looked so mature. Boom. I jumped up and found that, once again, I killed a jake. I hate them. It was still a lot of fun though.

Kill 16 March 30, 1994 – Coosa County (Rolling Place)

On sudden notice, Dad and I had to leave Swampy Acres. We weren't too upset. After all, we were four for four. Not bad! The idea of going to chase some Coosa birds in a way delighted us. Killing a turkey in swamp bottom is joyful. Digging one out of the Coosa hills is a hard-earned accomplishment the way turkey hunting ought to be.

The first day we tried to coax in Hugo [Hugo was a famous gobbler we hunted for years and never killed]. Another check for the bird. Hugo is building quite a reputation among the Henderson team. The second morning brought a frost. Dad stayed to try, once again, and outwit the legend. I was drawn to the Rolling Place and roosted one there the night before.

I parked, got my gear, and headed to listen. I wasn't carrying heavy 3 ½-inch fire power. Not even a 12-gauge. I even left the modern substance known as plastic behind. Two 16-gauge paper shells sat waiting in the chambers of the turkeyest gun there ever was – the L.C. Smith double barrel. Little did he know (nor did I) that he was about to bark.

At 5:15, I called – nothing. At 5:16 he couldn't help but sound off after I broke the silence again. He was 100 yards away down from me. He might've been roosting in the tree Dad had sat at and killed one the previous year. I eased in the small pine woods and found a fairly good place. Realizing I had forgot my hat, I placed my left shoulder aimed directly at the turkey to hide behind. My little box made some good tree calling, but no gobbling. After three minutes, dogs off in the distance brought him to attention again as his dominance sang throughout the land. Then, even as dark as it was, I heard his wings carry him down out of bed.

My fly-down cackle quickly followed to give him a reason to come. I scratched in the leaves to further entice him. Then the dogs barked again and he gobbled. I called so pretty on the true double, but no answer. He gobbled four times more in the next five minutes. He wasn't far, but still where he had flown down. Then silence. I had L.C. looking. After a few minutes – chuck varoom. In a few moments my circulatory factory turned on high speed and pumped my body full of adrenaline. The heavy breathing started. Here came the shakes. Over the sound my body was producing, I heard a few steps right in front of me. He appeared briefly, only exposing parts of his head through the thick mass. Boom boom boom boom boom boom – I was losing it. Where was he? He had disappeared behind the small tree and became silent. Three minutes past. Had he slipped off? I calmed down. Then I heard the leaves again. Here he came. He was close. As soon as he let me, I would shoot. He stopped with just enough clearing for L.C. to throw his action. At 15 steps, the turkey's life ended the way it should end. Coosa had brought forth another of the richest reward. At 2 o'clock in the afternoon, Coosa exposed herself again. Dad missed a big one with the new Ithaca 16 at 32 steps. Just one of those things where man's power cannot always defeat Coosa. She's awful tough. Novices, keep away.

Kill 17 April 26, 1994 – Hale County (Swampy Acres)

I've called up more turkeys in the past two years than I ever imagined possible. Monday came after the MCAT test and a one-week recess of hunting [MCAT is the Medical College Admissions Test to which I dedicated the week before studying instead of hunting], so I was ready to hit the woods (or fields in this case). I went to the backside of Chandler early, but heard nothing. Finally at 7 o'clock, I rounded a corner of growth and saw five or six turkeys in the fresh-plowed Greenridge. They weren't but 50 yards away, and they didn't run. The big dude gobbler just stood there while the hens kept feeding. I backed up, parked and snuck around to the other side of the field. As I got around to where they were, I saw one strutting with a brother at his side. No hens. If they were alone, I would surely have them. They were working their way to the left, so I sat at a tree down that way. I sat close but couldn't see the field because I was lower. A few minutes later, a train's horn coaxed one into gobbling. I called, but nothing. I called again loudly. I needed to hear him answer, but nothing. I couldn't stand not being able to see them, so I finally had to peek. I got on my knees and raised up. There he was – close. He was about 50 yards to my left and walking towards the woods. I ducked back down, wondering if I had spooked him, and spun around the tree to aim down the woods where he was. I was 10 yards from the field on one side and five yards from a swamp on the other. If I could call him up, he'd feed through the sliver of woods and right into my lap. I called – nothing. Then I saw him in full strut about 75 yards down. I thought I saw the other big boy with him. For the next 15 minutes, he strutted back and forth at that spot. I tried purring, clucking, yelping, and even being silent to bring him in. Then the hens showed up – problems. For 10 more minutes, the mother hen and I exchanged words. Non-stop cutting and yelping back and forth could not bring her or that displaying tom in. Eventually the turkeys moved on off. After driving around to the other side of them and trying for 15 minutes or so, I had to leave for school. My afternoon was open, and I planned to go back after them and maybe roost them for the next morning.

Well, in the afternoon I did just that. I started working the woods where they had been that morning, making my way slowly towards the top of the Greenridge. As I entered the last finger of woods, I saw five turkeys – looked like gobblers – running on the other side just outside the woods to my left. I had spooked them. After five minutes of being mad, I realized that those turkeys would come back in the fields in a short time. Those turkeys love the fields and will come back out even after being spooked. I eased across to the other side and set up on the edge behind some thick vines so I could only see the left corner of the field and the right side. The center was out of view. In 10 minutes as planned, I saw three gobblers come out over by the road to Swain. Then I saw a hen come out in the corner to my left. I watched them for a few minutes and decided to peek and check the center. There were two longbeards about 80 yards out. They were walking to the right. The afternoon went on and I couldn't get them interested. I watched the turkeys, three jakes and two big boys, walk over to roost on the swamp on the other side. About 15 minutes before fly-up time, something spooked them, and they ran into the corner by the road. I knew they would roost there, so I left. It turned out to be Trent Owens on a four-wheeler that spooked them. We chatted a while.

Morning came, Tuesday, and I was in the woods early near the road. I set up at a great tree and aimed towards the field and swap. I figured he'd roosted there and would pitch down in the field. Then I would have them. It was 5:40. I started calling with all my calls to sound like several hens. At 5:45, he gobbled on the swap back towards Swain. I was tempted to move closer, but stayed to keep the field in sight. I swiveled on the tree, now aiming back towards Swain. I continued tree calling. At 5:50, he gobbled again. Then a rough gobble on the swamp closer. They started gobbling good then. Jakes began gobbling all around. I could distinguish the older birds, and they were further away. It was time to make sure they flew down on this side of the swamp. I began doing some nice yelping with some cutting every now and then. I was careful not to call too much. The older birds gobbling died off quickly as I could tell they had flown down. They were moving away, but since I could still hear them, I knew they weren't far away in these bottomland woods.

At 6:15, the gobbling had stopped. Some sprinkles of rain came, and I was tempted to walk the road in search of those two big boys. I forced my-self to stay knowing they could be slipping up. I made the right decision. After 10 minutes, I checked the field. I saw the two longbeards entering the field by the road. Oh boy! I was hidden enough to spin on the tree and face the field. I gave a sweet yelp on my box which they must have liked. They headed my way. Oh, they looked so good! Their heads were blue and white and with long beards! I was ready to bring one to an honorable death as soon as they were in range. I let them come closer. There was a big tree just in front of me, so when they went behind it, I got ready for them to step out on the other side. Chuck-varoom, chuck-varoom. Oh my gosh! And they appeared. The lead's head went up, but I couldn't shoot due to a stick. What is he seeing – me? Please no. I was so sick of turkeys seeing me (mostly in Coosa County). His head went down as he stepped little closer. He was close so I took a shot. Got him! The other took off.

It was a really nice kill for my fourth of the season. But something was missing – Dad. There's nothing like hunting with Dad. Dad had been having a rough season with the Coosa birds. He tried harder than I've ever seen him, but they wouldn't come in. I had really hoped that Dad could get one to reward his time, but turkeys are turkeys. Dad fought hard, but all the Coosa birds beat him (and me). If Dad had been with me today, we could have taken both. That's something that we've never done. It's now a top goal of mine. Dad, you're #1.

Kill 18 March 29, 1995 – Hale County (Swampy Acres)

The 1995 season rolled around, and as usual, I was eager to spend time chasing turkeys. The year was cold all the way until three days before season when it got warm and stayed warm. Spring had come. My first four days were spent at Triple C with gobbling every day. In fact, the second morning, my listening spot turned out to be in gun range of two young gobblers.

It was dark and I eased down by a small tree in the edge of the cutover while they putted at me. I was still. Then they started gobbling. I could've easily taken the closest who had a nice beard, but why degrade him? They flew down out of range and the next three of five days were spent chasing them around. No score. Spring break came. Dad and I both needed a rest from our work and school. No luck in Coosa County, so we headed to Swampy Acres. As we drove through the Gray field on Saturday afternoon, two were strutting on the edge by the swamp with hens 100 yards away and they didn't run. I roosted them that night, but the next morning had no luck with them.

Monday, I went to Lynn Bottom. It rained – no luck though turkeys were gobbling everywhere. During both days, Dad and I both heard around 12 different turkeys. It was neat. Both mornings, Dad had worked a group of four that all gobbled their heads off together. Tuesday, I went to Gin House where Dad had been going and worked the same four (turned out Dad was on the other side working them also). Neither of us had luck. These four turkeys were roamers.

Dad worked them the first day over the creek between Gin House and Keaton fields, the second day by Gin House swamp, and the third morning again over the Keaton creek. We saw them on three separate occasions too; once all strutting with hens in the JT field, once driving around behind Lynn Bottom going to Keaton, and once standing tall in Lynn Bottom, all on different days. These turkeys were roamers, not real interested in hens, and Dad and I were now sick of them. Tuesday night we roosted a loner, a single gobbler in the same place every morning, just above Gin House field, and another single halfway down Keaton on the left. I wanted a turkey bad after hunting nine days in a row with gobbling each day. Dad had already taken a nice 14-pounder (not a jake) from Triple C. My time was due.

Wednesday morning, we woke at the new lodge – what a place! At 4:55, I eased down the left side of Keaton field. Dad went after the loner. Mine gobbled early and close. I slipped in and had a hard time finding a good tree close to the field. I couldn't move around too much as he was close, so I settled for a tree 25 yards from the field. He didn't gobble much, and flew down quickly. No more gobbling. I got ready. Then, way out down Keaton field I saw a black dot. It disappeared and then our four buddies came into view. They were at least 300 yards out. I yelped real loud – they stood up and then a mass of gobbles came my way. Then they started running straight towards me. They disappeared behind some trees – I got ready. Oh, how ready I was to take one with the new Winchester. Finally, there they were at 40 yards on the edge of the field walking to the right. The second had a good beard. They came to a good opening, but if I shot then, I would kill two and I'm against that. Finally, I shot on the second one. Boom!!! Got him! It was a great turkey. Later, Dad told me that when I shot, he had one very close. He wanted so bad to meet me at the intersection with one over his shoulder too. Our time will come, however.

Kill 19 April 1, 1995 – Coosa County (Taliaferro Farm)

There ain't nothing like killing a Coosa turkey. Thirteen days in a row of hunting. Thirteen days of gobbling. But it was time for a break, so the 14th day of the season, Dad and I slept in at home. I woke up, mowed the grass, laid around until we ate lunch. Then we headed to Coosa County for an afternoon hunt. We arrived at the farm at 2:50. We walked to the top field and separated. I went to set up in our spot while Dad backtracked to walk the loop.

Forty-five minutes went by of soft calling but there was no response. Then I decided to give a louder, more aggressive series of calls. Still nothing. Off in the distance, I heard Dad yelp. He yelped again and hobble-obble-obble, right in front of me probably 100 yards. Dad yelped again and got him going. Not knowing where I was or if I had heard the turkey, he crow-called for me, but I signaled back that I wasn't about to move. Thirty minutes went by of gobbling, silence, and walking, but I worked him in. It was a tough shot through a narrow opening of the brush. I was also turned around to my left and my arms were very tired. But the three inches worth of magnum powder and 2oz. of shot sent at least one #6 into his head. It was a great kill with all the elements: silence, gobbling, walking, strutting, waiting, all the while Dad listening off in the distance!

I want to thank God right now for that moment and for my times in the woods with Dad. Spending Spring Break in the woods was very relaxing for the two of us. We are both under a lot of pressure. He at work, me at school, but God offered us the opportunity to ease our minds and pursue his creation. Dad is my best friend. I also think he is the best dad in the world. While at times I may get frustrated, mad and short with him, I love him and hope he forgives me. It has been harder for me to hunt with him this year and I know why. I've become a young, eager hunter always disregarding personal comfort for the chance at a gobbler. Dad has accumulated many years in the woods and while just as eager to bring one down, he has learned when to take it slow, move on, or stay seated. He is a wise hunter, something that will take me time to reach. I love hunting with Dad and especially killing turkeys with him. This year, I want to watch him kill a good turkey, so I pledge my patience to stay with him and his companionship. And a final and more important note – I thank God for Dad and bowing our heads over the turkey and giving Him thanks. God deserves all the glory!

Kill 20 April 8, 1995 – Pickens County (Triple C)

After a nice spring break with Dad, I was determined to take one from Triple C. The next week, I heard much gobbling but couldn't do anything. Friday afternoon, I hunted the Cotton Field. I watched three gobblers and, after spooking them, roosted them. Dad came that night and we stayed in Tuscaloosa together. He didn't get much sleep. Saturday morning we slipped in by the field and set up. However, the turkeys I roosted were no longer in the trees where I had roosted them in. We heard gobbling on middle road and maybe Johnny [Jonny was a gobbler we'd hunted several times in the area], but not the ones I roosted. We stayed a while and watched three turkeys that looked big across the field. We decided to go after Johnny at 8 o'clock. We pulled down Shag road and heard Johnny gobbling over by Bob's fields. But as soon as we headed towards him, he stopped. We set up in his area for an hour, but nothing. It was a beautiful day, little wind, sunshine and dogwoods were in full bloom. There were two problems. It was getting hot (in the 80s), and it hadn't rained good since turkey season started (three weeks). Things were dry, which seemed to be shutting them down. At 10 o'clock, we headed to Dad's road. Sneaking up to the first field, we stumbled upon a gross four to five-foot snake laying across the road. It didn't move after we threw sticks at it, so we began to think it was a rubber snake and a Shag trick. He finally slithered away. I hope I never sit down on one or have one slide up to me! [Shag was a particularly loathsome turkey hunter at the hunting club who stooped to low levels to keep the competition, in this case us, out of his prime areas.] Halfway down to the second field, a hen cut loose. She sounded to me to be in the woods ahead, but Dad thought she was in the field below. We eased off in the bushes and short pines just in case. She kept yelping some. I still thought she was in the woods – Dad in the field. Dad kept asking if he heard drumming, but I wouldn't give him an acknowledgment. Finally, I made us head to the bottom in the woods. Just before the bend in the lower field, we heard cluck – yelp – yelp, right in the field. We turned around and headed in the woods to our right. You can't really set up in short pines but we nestled up on a small tree by bushes. The bend in the road was 20 yards in front of me. I aimed at the road, Dad through the woods and bushes towards the field. Due to the thickness of the pines, any turkey coming would surely follow the road.

We immediately heard drumming in the field. The next 20 minutes there was more drumming. We yelped some lightly and then he got going once again. His gobble was messed up – unable to be heard probably more than 50 yards away. But he was probably 30 yards away with the thicket between us. At times, there was walking in the thicket in front of Dad, and he was ready if he came that way. Finally, there was a drum further to the left, and we knew he was coming on the road. I got ready. He came marching around the bend – prettiest head I've ever seen. He was tall. I saw a long beard and locked the bead on him. He was walking – close. Too close to wait for him to stop for a standing shot. I took him!

He maybe flopped his wings twice – was graveyard dead. I shot him low and took out half his beard. Dang it! It was a longbeard. But Dad gathered all the shot-off pieces to put back together. I'm planning the reconstruction this summer. For now, the beard is 11 ¼ inches, but I placed one of the separate pieces up to the intact beard and it might be longer. I'll have the results later. It was nice having Dad pull one in for me with his keen little hen box. Also, the turkey had been shot earlier in the season with copper plated number sixes (mine were nickel-plated). He was body shot, and I believe this must have messed up his gobble.

Kill 21 November 21, 1995 – Clay County

Winter season of my last year in college came and I left early for the Thanksgiving holidays. I drove down and spent the night by myself at LBV Monday night. Tuesday morning I planned to go up to WW Ridge.

The temperature that morning was in the low 40s – not bad. I parked and peeled a juicy, succulent orange for fuel. Then, armed with the Winchester in one hand and a flashlight in the other, I climbed that mountain. Big trees were down everywhere from a recent hurricane. I veered more left than normal and found that over there, the ridge sloped down to the bottom. I made my way up to the top (now going parallel with the road). On the way up, I noticed a close ridge to the left of me. I decided to sit around there. I found a big oak and prepared its site. I kicked out leaves and rocks with my boots. I sat down and prepared my tools. I took my hat off and put my head net on. I took my gloves off to pull out my calls. Finally, I had to get my feet situated right. I dug out slots for my heels to fit in snuggly. And then, I swung my gun all around to check for swinging ability. There was a small tree in front that, in order to get my gun by, I had to compress my body back into the tree. I put my legs down and gun down too.

The sky was getting light but still 10 or 15 minutes from talking time. I decided to search the tree tops for any dark objects. I started scanning and immediately picked up a breast with a beard hanging down and a head sitting up top in a pine tree 20 yards in front of me. The silhouette gave me the impression of a small 1 ½-year-old. He wasn't looking at me. How – after all that movement I just did? I watched him for the next 10 minutes walk around and preen himself. He would stretch his neck out long to look around, but he didn't pick me up. A turkey started yelping close to my right and another at the bottom of the hill to my left. I was in the center. The one to my right flew down and hit 20 yards in front of me. He looked like a jake – then I saw a six-inch beard. Oh boy. Then the tree turkey flew down the hill out of sight. I had to take the smaller gobbler. Problem – my gun was on the right side of the tree in front and he was to my left in plain sight watching me. Somehow, I slowly maneuvered my gun over and got my head down. A lot of twigs and limbs were in the way so I had to wait for a better shot. Finally, he walked a little right. There were still twigs and his head was down, but I locked on and shot. I jumped up and immediately saw all the turkeys flush – including mine. He got up quick and by the time I pump and shouldered, he was 40 yards away in flight straight away from me. I folded him with the back-up # 2s. Upon inspection, he had no (and I mean none – zero) pellets from my first shot anywhere on him. I had totally missed. I still don't know how. I believe only # 2s got him. The first which broke his wing and sent him to a 40-yard fall down the hill and the other hit in his back. This was my first Fall longbeard.

Kill 22 March 22, 1996 – Clay County

What a late spring. It is been one of the coldest and longest winters I can remember. Opening day, it snowed on me and in the afternoon I saw a drove of turkeys at the Rolling Place. Three were strutting, but I couldn't do anything with them. The next day was an OK day, but I heard no turkeys. Spring just wasn't even thought of yet. It felt like I was fall hunting.

That afternoon, I drove the mountain loop in Clay County. On my last stop, I checked Mark's field. Way across on the other side, I saw about 15 turkeys. I couldn't get close to them, so I eased up the ridge in the woods just to watch them. I didn't really want to bushwhack one – as everyone calls it now. That ain't no fun. A turkey deserves a more honorable way to die than an ambush in the field. So I watched those turkeys for 3 ½ hours. There were eight hens, three jakes, and four big boys. I called a little, but they demonstrated no interest. Three had great long beards and the other had an eight or nine-inch beard. Finally, at roost time, they marched up in the woods straight at me. The lead one came 10 steps in front of me. He kind of noticed me, so they went around and up the ridge behind me. Yes, that's right – I didn't shoot. I let them walk. My grace was granting one of them one last night of sleep. And, when it all came to be, it was indeed one's last night of sleep. I got up in there early in the morning, way before light. I set up and when light broke, a jake yelped behind me, and I switched sides on the tree. I heard three turkeys fly down plus walking. So I laid out some sweet hen sounds. The walking got louder. Then one appeared very close – 50 yards and walking to my right. I had to turn him. He got out of sight over the ridge side and I let some more sweet music out. His walking got more to my right. I got my gun up left handed. He came up at 26 steps, I clucked to send his head up high looking for me. All I can say is – got him!

Kill 23 April 3, 1996 – Pickens County (Triple C)

That damn old woods line turkey. He had given me plenty of hell in 1995. He liked to gobble, just not move. Once last year, I positioned myself in the perfect and situation on him. His hens had flown down behind me, 30 yards. They scratched and yelped. He flew down 50 yards in front of me, down the ridge where I couldn't see him. One hen flew down with him. For two hours, I had my gun ready. I'm sure that plenty of times he was in range if only I could have seen him. He drummed solid for two hours. Then he slipped away. He gave me hell once this year. I worked him from five till noon only leaving him for an hour and a half.

He liked to gobble and strut. But these things he does no more.

After hunting with Dad on his road one morning, he left and I stayed to hunt some more. After getting nothing to happen, I headed back to the truck on Tub's road, but stopped to sit by a small pine tree by the road. I sat more to rest than to kill a turkey. I yelped softly. In five minutes, I heard walking in front of me. It was definitely a turkey. I put my head net on and got ready. The walking got closer. I got the gun ready left handed. Finally, I had my gun pointed where I expected him to pop out on the road. He did, but my gun wasn't on him. I barely saw his red wattles through the thick stuff. Then I saw his feathers puff up and he drummed loud. He turned the other way and started strutting that direction. I clucked. He drummed. I clucked again, afraid he was leaving. Then – here he came, marching mad as hell. But he had left the road to come into the woods on my side. He was close and my gun was way left of him. He stopped to drum, then marched on some more. I had to risk moving my gun because he was now almost behind me. I knew my opportunity would be over soon. He went behind a small tree – I swung. I was on him. He was marching, I clucked, but he kept marching. I yelped, but he wouldn't stop. It was now or never.

I got him.

I was so shook up that I had to lay down to get my senses and strength back. I had killed that damned old woods line turkey. I had killed him. The battle flags went up in my favor.

Miss 4 April 9, 1996 – Pickens County (Triple C)

Dang. Dad and I set up on one gobbling down off the middle country road. Didn't gobble too good. Got silent. Dad got up, and I went up to another one. I walked back down the road – heard walking off the ridge. I sat and up came a gobbler. I wasn't on him – he was close. He strutted about 15 yards. I tried to move the gun on him. He spooked and walked away – I took a potluck shot and missed. When I jumped up and shot, I folded him out of the air. He ran off over a ridge – I threw two more at him. Just disgusting – he became wildcat meat. A terrible, terrible thing!

Kill 24   April 9, 1996 – Pickens County (Triple C)

April 9, 1996   Winchester Mod. 1300
3:00 P.M.   Win. XX Mag 3" #6
Triple C – cotton Field   Jake
              Turkey #24

I succombed. I ambushed him. Dad + I had snuck up on 3 gobblers in the dry leaves. They saw us baraly + started looking. I saw one was a jake, but I eared in on one that looked like the famous cotton field turkey that couldn't be killed. This would be the only way to kill him. Dad said to shoot him, so I eased my gun up + drew down on him. Dang it – he was a jake.

Extra – I had missed + wounded a nice one that same morning

Kill 25   April 16, 1996 – Clay County

Lesson # 1 – The Proper Way to Kill a Turkey

When the sun begins to light up the eastern sky, get in the woods where you think turkeys are. Locate yourself on the highest point to listen for a gobbling turkey. Usually at a spot like this, ridges will come together. Whichever way one gobbles, you can ease down one of the ridges to him. As the sky becomes lighter, hoot like an owl, a barred owl, and make the hoot as realistic as possible with your mouth. If one does not gobble at it, wait a few minutes and try again. Keep this up until you make one gobble. If one does not gobble and it has become light enough for you to see to walk well, try calling on a box. Start with a light yelp and listen. Then fly-down cackle. Listen. Try a loud yelp. When he gobbles, he may sound far away down one ridge. Walk his direction on the ridge to where the ridge begins to slope steeply down. Call to make him gobble again. Now he'll sound a lot closer. Ease down the hill about 75 yards. Call again to make sure you're not too close. When he gobbles, you might realize you're pretty close. Look for a tree close by and duck while going to it. Turkeys up in trees can see for a long ways. If your tree isn't perfect – such as a small dogwood growing in the right hand side of the swinging path of your gun – make him gobble with a call to see if you can move. This will also let you know if you've already spooked him. If he doesn't answer, try again. If he still doesn't answer, it does not necessarily mean you've spooked him. Stay put. Give three minutes and call again. No answer again may mean nothing, may mean he's coming, or may mean he's spooked. Listen for drumming. If you hear drumming, he's not spooked and fairly close. Keep your eyes peeled. Hopefully you can spot him in the open woods as far as 100 yards. If you do and he's coming, don't call. He'll probably start gobbling and strutting as he looks for you. It is even possible you might see a couple of other mature gobblers with him. But, if only one has been gobbling, I doubt their heads will be lit up and blue as his. Enjoy listening to his gobbling and drumming and watching his beauty as he struts. At 50 yards, he may "hang up." Here, he stops to gobble and strut so as to find you. Don't say a word and don't shoot. He's too far. Be patient. After a while, if it looks like they are leaving, give a cluck. Be still, they'll look hard for you.

Give them a minute, they'll come marching. If he goes behind a big tree, get your gun ready on the left side. Trees down 25 yards in front of you provide good cover, but are bad to shoot through. Let him walk on around it for a clean shot. Be careful though, when he steps out, his buddy might be right beside him. Try to pick a shot where it will only kill one. If your turkey flops a lot and looks like he might get away, pounce on him and grab his neck. You now own him. Relish the victory.

Kill 26 April 24, 1996 – Clay County

Well, I did it. Got my limit. And what a beautiful day it was; the best of season so far. I walked my butt off. I got above Mark's field before day-break. At 5:53, one gobbled toward up towards Daddy Jake Mountain. I could tell he was far, but I had to go. I finally decided he was just over the end of the ridge that the cabin is on. I climbed it – in five minutes. Talk about something that will wear you out. At the top, I unfortunately found out that he was on the other side of the creek. I had burned up my legs for nothing. Walking back down the hill, my legs felt as strong as jello – and I knew what lay ahead. I was planning the hardest hunt of my life. Any hunt in Clay County ain't easy, but today I planned on walking and yelp-ing for hours. I was going to find one gobbling somewhere. By 10 o'clock, I had managed to climb four monster ridges while covering more than that many miles too. The only connection I had with turkeys was watching three fly off. Next on the agenda, I headed to where I knew the turkeys were – behind Willie Wilson's Ridge.

It was 10:30 when I climbed yet another death-defying ridge. I eased down the other side and set up. I dozed and yelped while reminiscing about the week before when I had one of my greatest textbook kills in the early morning. After an hour of silence – which was really surprising considering the stillness in the air and some of the prettiest calling ever – I decided to go in deeper and check out that green field I had seen up on top of the next ridge. More walking. I eased into the field and gave a loud yelp on my hen box. Gobbleobbleobbleobble – almost on top of me off the right side of the field and down. I hit the woods to the left. As usual, I jumped between trees never liking each one I found. I yelped – nothing. Ten minutes went by – nothing. I was getting worried that I had spooked him. I desperately wanted him to gobble again so I could switch trees – again. Finally he did, in the same spot. I switched and switched again. I was expecting him to come up skirting the edge of the field. He gobbled a couple of more times and I yelped again. Shortly I heard walking to the left of the field. He was definitely coming but circling first. Chuck-varoom. There he was, way to my left. He was about 60 yards and I barely saw him through the trees. He was moving left. I could hear lots of drumming. I needed to yelp to help turn him. He did turn around. He gobbled once and started coming. He was now angling to my right. He did just what I wanted. He hit the road leaving the field and came straight up. He got close and I took him at high noon. I gave him the honor he was conceived to receive. Even more, I gave God the honor for the blessing in my life. How merciful he is.

It is the end of a long and hard winding road. I set out early in my life, afflicted with the disease, to attain a goal. I wished to battle many a wild turkey. Wars were waged with winners each time. I was usually the loser. But defeat by a majestic blue head has left me satisfied when I leave the woods, but only to fuel my inward burning flame of desire. This desire to possess surpasses a simple wish to do something. It climbs higher than a liking to do something. Why I turkey hunt cannot be easily explained. It has been described as a need. But this seems also to understand my desire. It would seem that I would hate it, as most people at my pace would. But the few of us are enlightened by the chase. The few of us in the Tenth Legion.

1st turkey, Age 12. After Dad and I split to listen, he hustled back to let me know he spooked a couple jakes off roost that flew in different directions and would be easy to call back. But he also heard another turkey gobbling further away. It was my choice for which we pursued. I chose to go after the jakes. After shooting, I jumped on and wrestled the jake until I had a hold of his neck, gripping with all my might until he stopped flopping.

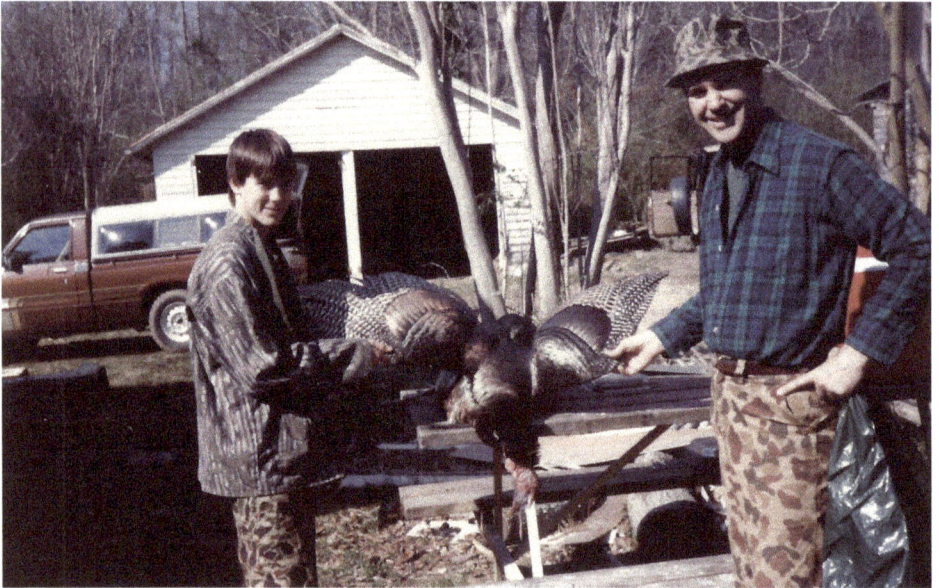

3rd turkey, Age 15. Pictured here with Dad. We explored some new private property in Coosa County, killing this turkey within an hour of being there. Despite killing this turkey so easily the first time we stepped foot on the property, after three decades of hunting there, these Coosa County turkeys have proved the most difficult of all turkeys we've hunted anywhere in the state.

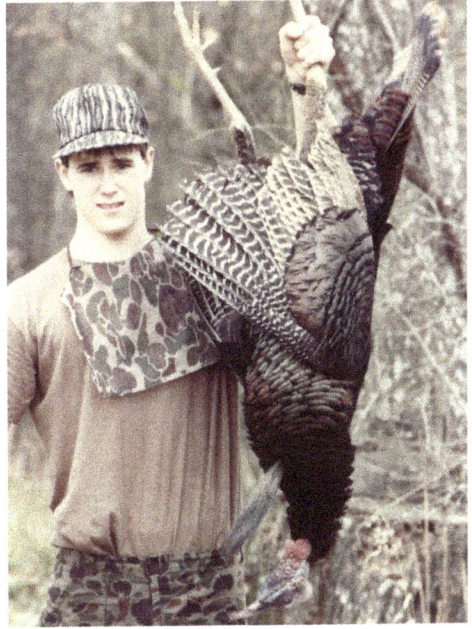

8th turkey, age 18. I killed this tremendous gobbler legitimately all by myself. I remember his facial features having watched him for 30 minutes – he was mean looking.

14th turkey, age 21. One of the few successful kills with a new Mossberg chambered for 3 ½-inch shells. Over several years, I missed more with this high powered gun than I killed.

19th turkey, age 22. A successful Coosa County hunt. Ain't no better way to carry a turkey out of the woods than over your shoulder with his wings flopping.

30th turkey, age 24. Despite the smiles, we ambushed these gobblers, dishonoring them. I would eventually grow wise and never succumb to such tactics again.

39th turkey, age 26. Success at finally killing a pair with Dad, sitting together and shooting at the same time. The success was dampened by unintentionally wounding a third gobbler in the group. During the event, we discharged several rounds of 3-inch magnums. Afterwards, Dad could never hear as well as it damaged his hearing.

52nd turkey, age 31. Killed this great Coosa County turkey in the woods with an old Ithaca Model 37 and blue Peters shell.

2007. Dad looking gruff in vintage camouflage holding the L.C. Smith 16-gauge, a weapon that's never missed over its career in both his and my hands.

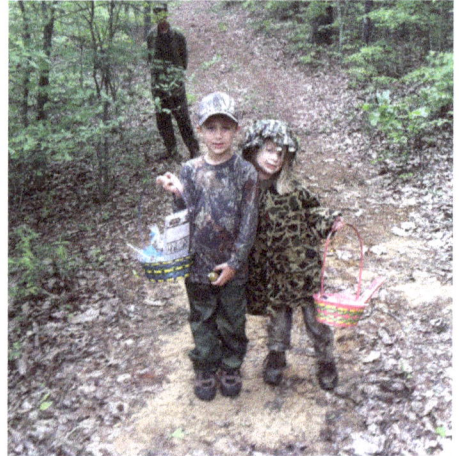

2011. Continuing the tradition of hiding Easter baskets in the woods for my kids as Dad did for me growing up.

2019. I'm still killing turkeys with vintage blue Peters shells. This gobbler had 1 ½-inch spurs, the best I've ever taken.

2019. Dad and I are still best friends and hunt almost exclusively together. Though he's a bit slower at age 77, we still chase turkeys around the hills in Coosa County among other places too.

2019. Dad's second kill for the season, a beautiful gobbler who ran around all morning gobbling before finally walking to the gun. Dad killed him with the old Ithaca 16-gauge using new TSS shot. We sat together at the same tree just like we always have.

87th turkey, age 46. A rare photo these days, as I don't often stop to take pictures with turkeys I kill anymore. Writing the stories of the hunts is more important to me.

REFINING THE ART

Following college, I started medical school at the University of South Alabama in Mobile and got married. New demands meant I could no longer hunt all I wanted, though I still found ways to hunt quite a lot. Over the four-year period, I found plenty of time to get back to our established hunting tracts in central Alabama whether it be on weekends or spring break to hunt familiar territory with Dad. We remained close despite the distance between us, communicating by phone or the new technology email about each and every hunt. We continued to hunt Clay County and the Coosa County properties a little, only killing a couple on the LBV Farm tract. I was starting to learn how much harder Coosa County turkeys were to kill than all the other areas we hunted. Triple C remained productive until we left the club after the 1998 season. It was around then that we discovered two fantastic new locations – another large tract on the Black Warrior River in Greene County (Cherokee Hollow) and a large mountainous tract in Shelby County. The Greene County tract was bottomland similar to the property upstream in Hale County, both holding large numbers of turkeys. Shelby County, in contrast, was a large tract of mountainous hardwood that became one of our all-time most productive locations.

In addition to hunting these new and old areas in central Alabama, I had to find some places to hunt in south Alabama near school. My first year there, I found the Boykin Management Area in Washington County which had some turkeys but was rampant with hunters. I managed to kill a great turkey there the first day I hunted it. And my last year in school, I found the newly state-purchased Upper Delta Management Area in Baldwin County which afforded me the most awesome and primitive habitat I've ever hunted. It was deep, remote, surrounded by rivers and epitomized the forest primeval where I've always envisioned turkeys evolved. It was in these river bottoms that turkeys remained during their near extinction in the early 20th century. It was in these river bottoms that my literary hero, Tom Kelly, learned to turkey hunt. And it was because of Tom Kelly, whom I befriended while there, in lending me his boat, that I navigated the rivers and killed two gobbling turkeys in the deep forest primeval.

Nostalgia percolates through the stories again with the occasional use of old blue Peters brand shells. Dad had been carrying around an old box of them for decades, ever since they were discontinued when Remington bought out Peters before I was born. The Peters 12-gauge shells were deep blue and a fascination to us – there was just something unique and awesome about chambering that blue shell to shoot a turkey. We also ended up buying an old Fox Sterlingworth double barrel 12-gauge to rival the L.C. Smith in antiquity. We managed to kill many turkeys with it.

Kill 27   March 20, 1997 – Washington County (Boykin Management Area)

How sweet it is. I really can't believe this actually happened. It is a new era in my life. I've just started medical school, and I thought my turkey hunting days were over. But God has blessed me, and I have done well. I am going to be able to get out more than I thought.

I scouted Boykin a couple of days before the season. Opening morning, I really didn't know where I wanted to go. I just settled for the train tracks, not expecting much. My preseason scouting had left me somewhat discouraged about this place.

The weather was worse than expected. There were some high winds and light rain that followed me in, but soon stopped. I listened a good ways down the road. As it got light, I was surprised to find some hardwoods that were scratched to pieces. Then one gobbled a good ways off. I got about 200 yards from him and got him to answer my yelp. By now, it was 6 o'clock, and I could hear other people working him too.

He started moving off, so I followed. I walked through another hardwood bottom that was scratched to pieces. All along the way, I would set up until he gobbled. Then, I would move closer. To my surprise, hidden by gallberry bushes, I was able to walk about 75 yards from where he was screaming. It was now 6:30.

I had been calling with my boxes. Then I yelped with my True Double. He loved it. From then on, he answered just about everything I threw at him. Then a hen got to yelping and cutting back at me. I figured I was dead. He'd never leave her. But he finally did. He came straight in, slowly, strutting and gobbling. I took him at 23 steps.

It was a great kill for me – a great way to start my first season while in medical school, to kill a gobbling South Alabama turkey, and a true blessing from God. Thank you.

Kill 28   March 28, 1997 – Pickens County (Triple C)

March 28, 1997   17.7 lbs
10:30 A.M.   10" Beard
Triple C - below F   1⅛" spurs
Ithica 28" - Peters #6   23 steps
       28th Turkey

Well, it was the best day of turkey hunting Dad and I have ever had. Finally, we each killed a turkey on the same day. Even greater, we were both together for both kills. And what makes it so awesome - they were both great kills.

It was a windy day that showed signs of possible rain. We drove from B'ham early that morning - Friday. And listened at 4-oaks - Nothing. So then we walked Tub's road. Finally we heard one way off. He ended up not being as far as we thought - the wind must have been dampening his gobble. We set up to him across some fresh cut over. Anyway, we called a little, he got silent, + then came up about 60 yds. He stayed there for 30 min. He didn't gobble much, but we did hear him drumming alot. Then, we pulled the hen he was with on over, he followed, and dad busted him. It was really great. (Time - 7:15)

We cleaned his, took pictures, and then went after one for me. After a while, we heard one gobbling a mile off. We were standing in P and he was way across on middle road. So we went. We did some walking - serious walking. But we got up on the turkey. It took about an hour - he never stopped gobbling for more than a minute. Dad got to watch him at 60 yds strutting + gobbling for about 20 min. Then, I clucked him in. He circled, came up close, + I maxed him. It was really really great. Then, the greatest part, Dad and I prayed + thanked God for the event. I love you Dad.

Kill 29 March 29, 1997 – Pickens County (Triple C)

Good grief – Dad and I have now killed five turkeys and it is not even April yet. Thank goodness he re-joined Triple C. We have been waxing them there this year, but so have the deer hunters. Deer hunters –they saw so many turkeys this past year that they got all fired up and have come out in droves to hunt our turkeys. They killed one opening weekend, got a jake the next Thursday, and missed a nice one too. Oh, I forgot about the miss on the turkey in full strut at 60 yards out in the Cotton Field. I think they are finally running down. But not after they screwed it up for us. Dad and I are turkey hunters – let us turkey hunt, we let you deer hunt.

Anyway, Saturday morning, due to the deer hunters pushing their way into our good areas, we listened down Dad's cutover road. Two started gobbling where they always do, towards the end but down by the creek and cutover. But they sounded to be out in the cutover or even across – and we blew it. My impatience had us hurrying too fast to the turkeys. Dad had some strange maneuver that – well, maybe it was mostly my fault. We walked right into them. Both flew away.

We left, hunted the rest of the morning, and then went back to converse with the deer hunters. The good thing about deer hunters is they can be good scouters for you. They let you know where they heard gobbling and where not. They are so full of it too. For some reason, they think turkey season got started so early this year that, and I quote, "you'll be lucky to hear a turkey gobbling on this property in 10 days." Since it's March 29, that puts the end of all gobbling on April 7 – yeah, right. That is the biggest bunch of bull – but I agreed with it all the way. The sooner they think season is over, the sooner we get Triple C all to our own – the way it should be.

About 10 o'clock, we slipped back in where we flushed the two early turkeys. It was a beautiful area. We yelped off and on for an hour – nothing; but it had been a pleasant sit with some napping. Before we got up, I gave my famous soft cutting – gobblobblobblobble – to our right, close, and down in the hollow. We spun. Nothing for 25 more minutes. I called lightly. Finally I heard walking. It was up above us. I got ready left handed. Then I saw him at 50 yards. He was looking hard. It was fun narrating for Dad because he couldn't see the turkey. But he came on down slowly.

I really wanted Dad to get him, but a tree was blocking his view. I finally decided not to risk him seeing us and took him. It was nice, but I still wish Dad had taken him.

What a season. It is now April 1. I haven't been for the past two days. I'm going to go Thursday. But I'm not going home this weekend. I need to study – and I'm dying to go – but I can't. I need to prepare for my future so I'll be able to hunt for the rest my life. Priorities.

Kill 30 April 17, 1997 – Pickens County (Triple C)

Here's my story. Dad and I called to three strutting turkeys on the other side of the Cotton Field for four hours. They had hens with them – nothing. It was the windiest day I have ever had.

We left and came back at 5 o'clock. We snuck up on the other side where they had been. There they were – about 40 yards. So what did we do – we ambushed them as they followed some hens closer. It was a pure disgrace. We shot two at the same time, never having even called. We were blinded by our desired to get a double ¬– and we dishonored two old turkeys by not engaging in a battle. We were the losers that day. We have made a vow – never will we ambush a turkey again!

Kill 31 April 20, 1997 – Shelby County

Who would've ever thought. I almost skipped going to medical school because I was afraid it might end my hunting for a good number of years. And I was ready for it too. So here I am now, with my longest beard ever, five mature turkeys for the season (one of which was taken less than honorably), and doing well in medical school. Who other than God can be given credit for my situation. Of all the turkeys I killed this season, of all the good grades I've made, the best of times were on a knee in front of a dead turkey praying to the Lord himself with my father.

This turkey kill was classic and beautiful. Double Oak Mountain is one of the most gorgeous solid stretches of hardwood I've ever been in. Hunting it is simply pure old woods hunting. And even more awesome are the little heads of the turkeys. They are great. [Dad and I've always associated smaller gobbler heads with purer wildness. Domestic turkeys, for example, have large heads.]

Anyway, we hunted the Long Ridge Road early. We heard one turkey gobble one time far off. We were surprised at the stillness in the air. The report when we left house was six mph winds, so we were expecting some winds high up on the mountain. But it was a good still day. Upon leaving, we decided to investigate Dwaine's careless claim of a gobbler living behind the tower. [Dwaine was the only other person to hunt the property in Shelby County. One of the first times we met him, he told us he'd been hunting a turkey behind a large cell phone tower in the middle of the property which… you will read] To this day, I bet Dwaine still finds himself vomiting in a toilet over that mistake. But he was right. We made one gobble down in there. We ran, got my gun and calls, and headed to him. I was planning on sitting atop the ridge, but luckily, Dad pointed out that we were atop a cliff that the turkey wouldn't be able to climb. So we somehow went scaled down the cliff. Dad was quite scared doing it. But we got down ok and set up. We were afraid the turkey could have seen us come over the cliff, so when he answered our second yelp, we were feeling mighty nice. In a little while we heard drumming. Then I saw him about 75 yards strutting. After some light clucking, we pulled him in. It was absolutely delightful.

This year, Dad sat with me at the same tree for four of my kills. That was great and brought back memories of the old days. I just hope I have as good a season sometime in the future.

Kill 32   March 22, 1998 – Pickens County (Triple C)

March 22, 1998
Triple C. — Woods between D+F
New Ithica 25" plain Barrel
Winchester 3" 2 oz #5

9:35 – time
Steps – 19
Wt – 19.5 lbs
Beard – about 8"
Spurs – not too bad

Turkey # 32

I've written before of new eras in my life, but none have been as dramatic as this most recent. I met a fine girl – beautiful, smart, loving, loves the Lord. I married her – last June. She's been traveling for work lately, and I've been doing a little hunting — I miss her. I have found that though turkeys are fun, challenging, and thought consuming, they are not fulfilling like my relationship with Kathy. I'm not a perfect husband, nor she a perfect wife, but that's our goal #1 – killing turkeys #2.

Two horrible opening days – windy and cold – though on the second Dad & I called one up strutting & gobbeling 25 yrds. Neither of us could get a good shot. Then he left.

Next morning got in some good gobbling. Met back with dad & we walked middle road to the other side. It was a georgus day. We sat & yelped for 10 in the woods off F. Then we set up in the woods off D. We heard one way off. It was 9 o'clock. Sounded like he was back where we had been calling off F. We headed to the next ridge & set up. He gobbled 7 or 8 times way off. I called sparingly. He shut up. 10 min passed when I saw him down in the hollow in front. He came up circling behind & to our left. I took him at 19 steps. Big turkey, what a kill!

Kill 33 March 23, 1998 – Pickens County (Triple C)

"Birds" here, "birds" there, "birds," as deer hunters want to call them, were everywhere. Boy, was I in the turkeys. During four separate occasions, called up a total of four jakes and three hens. I worked one gobbling all morning long. He was down off the north side of the end of middle road – I was down off the south side. Absolutely gorgeous woods. I was hearing turkeys everywhere – including one pretty close over by the pasture. But I followed this one, always trying to get around in front of him (he was working his way towards the end). The last spot I set up was close to the end. He was getting close. I could hear him drumming (and walking I thought). Suddenly, to my right and close – goobbblllleee!!!

Oh, what was I going to do? In order to get ready for that turkey, I would have to get my gun up left handed. But I had to be ready right handed for this other who was going to pop up at any moment to my left. So I kept my eyes peeled to the right. There he was. Coming down the road – strutting. He was 35 yards. He walked behind a couple of trees. I risked it and turned my gun around. Oh, I was so glad to hear him drum after that. He stepped out. I now own him. Turned out, Dad had slipped in and was just about to kill that other one. I wish he had.

Kill 34 April 12, 1998 – Shelby County

We just keep killing 'em. It was so easy. This time, Nick (my brother in law) tagged along. We listened and hunted the ridge top road – walking two or more miles. Boy, is it beautiful. We saw some tracks, just heard nothing. Nothing at all. So we road hunted on the way out. The last place we went was that westernmost road. Nick and I let Dad off while we eased ahead in the truck 200 or 300 yards (Dad was putting out our Easter baskets). We drove down a ways and saw a big gobbler running down the road – so we backed up (and caught Dad putting out our Easter baskets). Nick and I eased down the road. A good ways down, I heard walking in the woods. Nick and I sat down. I called – one gobbled a good ways away. So I summoned Dad and we headed after him. We eased off the road and set up. He had been gobbling. I called some and he got hot. Then silence. Finally I heard walking. There he was – running up. He stopped to strut a second and came on in. I took him at 25 yards. Fun, but I've had better.

Kill 35 April 20, 1998 – Pickens County (Triple C)

Dad and I both concluded this was the longest we had ever stayed in the woods on one day. We entered the woods in middle country around 5:45, worked a turkey till 7:30, eased around the whole property till 2 o'clock, and got back in the truck at 2:30. Despite the five turkeys we heard gobbling at roost, we couldn't even find a turkey to spook, let alone make gobble, for six hours. Absolutely nothing. So we got in the truck, drove down to check Dad's secret road, then headed back out. We passed the spot we had parked that morning (road leading to F), and while passing the road to that small green field on the right side, I heard a gobble just outside the truck (my window was open). I looked over and saw a big turkey standing just off the road leading to the field. So here we were driving, after not being able to make a turkey gobble for four hours and one gobbles at us in the truck. We pulled off the road, 100 or so yards down and prepared our gear.

For the next hour we worked him. He didn't gobble a lot, but some. He was in the field. We were set up on the edge of the main road about 60 yards from the road to the field. After 20 minutes of silence and a gobble that sounded like he had moved way off, we snuck to a couple trees by the road entrance to the field. I cut to make him gobble so we could get a read on where he was headed – gobbblllleee – right down in the field. We got ready. He was drumming. It took another 30 minutes, but I finally pulled him up the road and shot him with the Ithaca 16-gauge. He just couldn't stand it. Turned out, he was down there with four hens – but I won!

Kill 36 April 21, 1998 – Coosa County (LBV Farm)

Wow, what a way to end the season and get my limit. I really like LBV now. I didn't used to. But now they gobble so well – and it is absolutely gorgeous there.

Dad and I headed out the door early to get to the Dogwood while it was still dark, but it was cracking more than we expected. On our way to the gate, I thought I heard a couple of gobbles. Dad told me the same thing – we laughed thinking it was car noise. Then gobblllleee – in the valley. It was so early – we were very surprised. So we crossed the field at the fence and listened at the woods. We heard two gobbling seemingly across Mr. Gilliland's pasture – but close enough to hunt. They weren't together, but about 300 to 400 yards apart. So we split, Dad went to the right one and me to the left. So I headed down, crossed the creek, and eased up the other side. Both turkeys were gobbling well. I got as close to the edge of the field as I thought I could. The turkey sounded like he was in one of the big pine trees just across on the edge on the other side.

Gobbbblllleeee – what a gobble he had. It was the longest drawn-out gobble I've ever heard. I had the new video camera with me, so I got some good gobbling on tape. I started to call. He got hot – hitting everything I threw at him. But I didn't call too much, a new tactic I learned last year and this year. I heard a hen between Dad's turkey and mine begin yelping and cutting for the next 15 minutes like I've never heard before. And Dad's turkey got so hot. Finally, I could tell mine flew down. He was down on the other side, blocked from view by the top of the field. So I moved closer to the edge of the field. I could barely hear him gobble. Normally I would not think I could call him from that far across the field, but I felt confident – right up to the point when a hen cut loose with him. So I called a little and waited. Suddenly, I saw him way over there on top the field strutting. He looked so good that I videotaped him. And he began gobbling good again. Then I saw another mature gobbler with him – not strutting or anything; then a couple of hens (after watching the video, I think they were jakes). So I called a little – he responded. All of a sudden he folded up and headed my way – the other mature gobbler following. I got ready. He gobbled once on the way – I yelped softly. Oh, I couldn't believe it – at LBV! I wanted him so bad! He kept coming straight to me. He was getting close to range, then he stopped and started strutting. Across the field the two jakes came running. He started looking closer than I had thought. I was wide open and so nervous he'd see me. And if he did, I'd be sick. So when he stuck his head up, I couldn't stand it. I'll let the new Ithaca 28-inch plain barrel, 3-inch XX magnum #6 load do its work. Boooooommm – oh no, he got up and started running to the right with the other turkeys. I got up and remember maneuvering around the barbed wire. They took to flight. He was probably 60 or 70 yards flying directly perpendicular from left to right – booooommmm! Got 'em! He folded. I jumped the fence, ran out there – he was historialized. Now I do hate that I missed him on the first shot and almost lost him, but it was awfully fun watching him fold out of the air. What a beard he had! What a beard!

Kill 37 March 28, 1999 – Greene County (Cherokee Hollow)

Not much time to hunt this season. I have started my school rotations and really only have spring break to hunt. Dad and I have been planning an extensive nine-day hunt together consisting of Dreamland BBQ, steak, O'Charlie's caramel pie, Cottonpatch fried chicken, veggies, initiating ourselves to Cherokee Hollow, back to Triple C, over to LBV, Clay County and the Farm. We had both bought bikes before season and planned to hunt off them. So we met Friday afternoon, March 27, at Cherokee Hollow to scout. What a gorgeous place. We biked around, hearing two gobbling at 5 o'clock, and watched four big gobblers out in front of the house.

Well, Dad got sick with the flu and stayed inside all Saturday and Sunday. Sunday morning, I went to the back property and heard seven gobbling. I was pumped. About 3 o'clock, I decided to slip down into the woods to the left of the house. When I got in the woods, I let my hustling hen loose – gobble gobble gobble – either two or three turkeys in front of me on the edge of the field. Probably about 200 yards. So I quickly found the tree. For the next 10 minutes, nothing. They wouldn't answer me again. Then, finally I saw a big gobbler heading towards me about 150 yards out. He gobbled once, never stopped to look for me, and headed to the field about 70 yards in front. He quickly crossed the field and started gobbling. I was disappointed he hadn't even given me a chance when – gobbbbllee – from where the other turkey had come from. Up came a beautiful gobbler – strutting and gobbling. He stopped about 75 yards out and sat there for 15 minutes looking, strutting, and gobbling. I tried to cluck him in but all he did was strut more. Finally, he started coming, but angling to my left. At about 50 yards, he stopped behind a big log, looked around, and decided to go and join his partner gobbling across the field. He never looked back. So when I heard him across the field, I took off to try and circle around in front. I eased into the woods at the tip of the field and sat down. At first yelp, he gobbled. In five minutes, I saw him coming. At 50 yards, once again, he froze. He sat in one spot for over 30 minutes strutting. He never gobbled again. Nothing I did would bring him in – not silence, not cutting, not clucking. I was dying. Then he slowly started easing away to my left. When he got far enough away so I could move (about 100 yards), I started scratching in the leaves. And that did it. He came right on in and I took him at 25 steps and 4:50 p.m. What a hang-up turkey! Good 11-inch beard.

Also, during the hunt I got very weak and blurry vision. Yes, I caught the flu from Dad.

Kill 38 March 29, 1999 – Greene County (Cherokee Hollow)

Elements that make up a great kill are the following:
- lots of gobbling including up close
- having the turkey close for a period of time and not being able to see him
- having hunted the turkey a previous morning and the more the better
- using tactical moves
- a turkey that looks good coming in with a vividly colored head standing tall at times

This turkey had many but not all of the above. It was really great. I got him going about 6:15. He sat out there at 150 yards for close to an hour. I tried clucking, soft yelping, loud yelping, purring, scratching, and even silence. He liked to gobble, but I just couldn't convince him. Finally, I'd had it. I poured it to him. He loved it. Every gobble was a little closer. He came in slowly but was always letting me know where he was. His gobbles at 30 yards were so strong. The under-gobble drum was awesome. A few seductive yelps brought him through the bushes into view. He looked good. I took him. All the while, Dad lay sick in bed. A little secret – I was sick too.

Kill 39 April 24, 1999 – Greene County (Cherokee Hollow)

Dad has had a rough season – very rough. After finally getting over the flu, he started back hunting three weeks into season. Boy, the turkeys have been at LBV, but they've been typical LBV turkeys – impossible to call. [I'm referring to Coosa County turkeys which have always been the toughest turkeys to call up, even to this day.] He chased them morning after morning and has grown real frustrated with turkey hunting. He gets lonely without me. Even two great days at Swampy Acres were discouraging. Swampy Acres has gone way downhill – there are not many turkeys there anymore. So we got one more chance to hunt together this year and decided to go to Cherokee Hollow. I showed up Friday afternoon at 4 o'clock, we got one gobbling behind the pines to the left of the horses. We even got him hot. We got so close to him. But he never would come. So next morning, we were standing right there – and it was dark. As I owled the third time, one gobbled on top of me. Dad joined up and we sat right there by the road. As daylight came we heard a couple others behind him gobble once in a tree, but they wouldn't gobble much. Finally we heard them gobble on the ground about 200 yards out. I laid some good calls on them and they started coming. Then we heard drumming. Finally, Dad saw them coming down the road. Then I saw them. So we were ready to get a double. Here they came. The first one stepped out about 18 yards and then one followed, but there was a lot of stuff in between us. We were prepared at any moment. So they stepped closer and were on top of us (later measured 15 steps). But by now those two were side by side and behind all kinds of limbs. It was getting to the point where we needed to shoot. Then a third came towering around behind them. Since those first two were behind limbs and next to each other, I instinctively pulled my bead to that third one. I counted one, two – boom. From that point it is kind of a blur. I saw my turkey go down but then get up and start flying away – I folded him. Then I heard Dad shoot again (even though I saw his flopping in the road). I looked left and the one he had shot at was running away. Apparently what happened is Dad hit that second lead turkey too. After I shot again, Dad noticed that the second one was bouncing up and down like he was wounded. Then all of a sudden he recovered and ran away. The thought of wounding one took something away from this. It was a great double but could have been better. I hate wounding one. If I had only stayed with and shot one of those two lead turkeys. We will know better next time. Dad needed this turkey bad. Both had 11-inch beards, but his was 15 ½ pounds. These were the infamous house turkeys.

Kill 40 March 20, 2000 – Baldwin County
(Upper Delta Management Area)

There ain't nothing like exploring new territory, and I don't think I'll ever find a place more fun to explore than the Mobile delta by boat. Rivers and creeks and logs and cypress trees. It is just awesome. I had six gobbling turkeys located the week before season. Opening morning came – nothing all morning – what a disappointment – until . . . I stopped on the south part of Douglas Lake and entered gorgeous woods on the right. I eased in and yelped. One gobbled down and across the river. I jumped back in the boat and crossed. The other side was low land. I crossed one small sliver of water (jumped across) and a bigger one (fell in while crossing on log). I kept him located with my crow call. I sat down, called him up, gobbling well, and shot him as a boat passed by.

Miss 5 March 27, 2000 – Greene County (Cherokee Hollow)

At least I didn't wound him. The third day we hunted him over in the park area. Got him gobbling in about 9 o'clock. He didn't gobble much this time. Silence – then he was on us to my left. Dad was at my right. I raised and shot. Don't even think I knocked him down. No feathers. He was gone flying quickly. Disappointing – especially since it was supposed to be Dad's. Well, Dad got him three days later. Saw two small shot wounds in his breast beginning to scab over from where I shot. He gobbled over 1,000 times in 4 ½ hours when Dad got him. Dang – I wanted him. Hooray!

Kill 41 March 28, 2000 – Greene County (Cherokee Hollow)

The first day that Dad hunted (LBV), he called one up and clicked his gun on a good turkey at 21 steps (no shell in gun). Yesterday, we called up a great one after three days of working him. He came on my side, and I flat out missed him at 20 steps. So I really wanted Dad to get one. Next day we went to the back country area and heard a disappointing nothing on roost. Finally, we heard one way off. We got closer and sat down. He gobbled two more times. Then a mature gobbler with a jake-size beard came running up on my side but out of range. A few moments later, Dad saw more coming. They were running where the other went. But some sweet, soft calling turned the mature looking turkey in. I had Dad swing his Fox Sterlingworth over in front of me to shoot. At 20 steps, Dad tried to shoot the turkey, but had left the safety on. All I saw was his barrel wiggling around from squeezing the trigger and trying to get the safety off which he couldn't. The turkeys saw it too, and I had to take him. Dad ended up getting a great one the next day. He gobbled over 1,000 times – we counted!

Kill 42   March 31, 2000 – Clay County

March 31, 2000
Clay County – Below Mark's Field
9:00

Screamer
#42

Fox Sterlingworth
High V #5 - Winchester
21 Steps
10½" Beard
Good Spurs

With Honors from Clay County! Dad's first spring in the mountains in probably 10 years. Nothing behind the N House. Then on to Mark's field. Below it, in the woods (we don't field hunt) we yelped & napped. After I woke up I heard a far off gobble. we ease closer to the field found a tree & sat. He gobbled fairly close in the field. Took about 20 min – 4 or 5 gobbles, drumming as he came in. 30 yds in front, he hopped up on a log & strutted. I took him a few steps later. Dad called it one of the most awesome ever! It was!

Kill 43 April 5, 2000 – Baldwin County
(Upper Delta Management Area)

I'm sitting here trying to write this story, but all I can do is watch this brilliant red bird outside the window. It isn't a cardinal – it is much redder. I have never seen a bird so pure and bright red. It is beautiful, much like the brilliantly colored head of a pure strain turkey under the dark delta canopy. And there was an element to this one that I have always wanted – water – specifically, wading water to get him. Sort of brings the duck hunting effect that I enjoy and applies it to turkey hunting – wading water. Water was everywhere. The rivers were rising from recent heavy rains. I launched the boat from Boatyard Lake. The fog was out, but I made it to Hogan's Bend ok. Then it got me. I had to stop and float along until I heard the creek where I was going to park rushing with the rising water. I was now late. As I approached the power line, one gobbled on the other side – right where I wanted to be listening – dang! I heard lots of flying down near him. I ran up the line to cross and hoped the fog would protect me. As I crossed the line, I hit water. That entire side was flooding. Where would I go from here? They had to go out into the power line as their side was flooded, but there was nowhere to sit over there. He never gobbled again, but I heard hens with him. I also heard a hen yelping her guts out behind me – across water. I walked around through three inches of water for 15 minutes and couldn't figure out what in the hell to do. I thought I saw some dry ground way through the woods near that yelping hen. So I did it. I waded across rushing water up to my knees – so much fun. Big trees on the other side. I sat at a giant oak with root armrests. Me and the hen yelped back-and-forth. I could see a mist all out through the woods and wondered if water was everywhere. She started getting closer. Then – gobbbbblllleeeeee! Right with her. She yelped more, then I saw a turkey fly from where the yelping was and land about 100 yards out. It was her. She yelped. I yelped back. Then another turkey flew and landed near her. It was him. He strutted. I lightly yelped. He looked and strutted again. The woods were so dark from the canopy, the trees were now green, the forest floor was covered with light green grasses and weeds, tall weeds with yellow tops were scattered about, water was flooding the land behind me and mist followed water all throughout the forest in front of me. I was between two arches of an oak base, his head was glowing blue – awesome! He came on in and I got him – killed that turkey dead. Boy, did he flop.

Walking back, the other turkeys were in the power line and the waters had risen further. Four for the season!

Kill 44 April 18, 2000 – Coosa County (LBV Farm)

Well, I did it. Got a good dose in before heading to North Carolina. Dad has hunted this place so hard and I came in and waxed one – I feel bad. I did what Dad will never do – get across to Mr. Gilliland's side early. Horrible day – very windy. Heard one off the property in that hunting club land. So I eased over and set up near the fence. In a little while, thought I heard walking across it but it went away. Then one way behind me gobbled a few times. Then across the field one gobbled – close. He gobbled three times. I heard walking. I got ready. Finally, he appeared – close (15 or so yards). I waxed him. Two others flew away. I don't think this was the one gobbling. Oh well. Limit for season. On to L.C. Smith 410.

LIMITED OPPORTUNITIES

After completing medical school in 2000, I went to North Carolina to further my training, a location far removed from my beloved Alabama hunting locations. The first-year internship was demanding and allowed me hardly any time to go hunting. In fact, I don't think I killed a turkey that year. But after ending my internship and entering dermatology, I was able to get back to Alabama on some weekends and properly timed vacations and great moments hunting with Dad. The Greene and Shelby County properties remained productive locations and Clay County saw a resurgence. Though I did hunt a few locations in North Carolina including the Uwaharrie National Forest, by and large, I never found many turkeys there and only called up one that I missed.

Kill 45 April 4, 2002 – Greene County (Cherokee Hollow)

I'm always writing about new eras, but two years in another state definitely qualifies as a new era. The decade of the 90s and including the year 2000 were unbelievably successful and left many memories to carry me through my residency in North Carolina. Internship was horrible and even worse, a great hindrance to my avocation during 2001. In fact, I hunted only five days total. Two days were spent back in Alabama and were remarkable only for calling up and meeting for the first time the Shelby Co. Power Line Turkey. He came close, in fact within sight at 60 yards, but then he left, walking far, far away.

Hunted three days in NC and did find a gobbling turkey in the Uwaharrie National Forest, but ran him off trying to get too close. This year, I'm still working hard and don't have much time to hunt, but Dermatology is a whole new world but allows me to keep up a hunting schedule.

March 29 to April 7, 2002 – a 10-day vacation for 10 days of hunting turkeys back in the great state of Alabama was awesome. Here's how it went:

Day 1 – turkey gobbled six times in bowl of Clay Co. – didn't come close to killing him

Day 2 – Loop Turkey that Dad missed the year prior on Lanny's property gobbled 10 times in rain – didn't come close to killing him either.

Day 3 – got the Shelby Co. Power Line Turkey gobbling at 7:30, gobbled well, but as always, he went away. He's a going-away turkey.

Day 4 – turkeys gobbling everywhere in lower woods of Cherokee Hollow. One went by at 50 yards, a big group walked out of hearing range, and got one gobbling in pasture next to Sci's at 9:00 – hard to believe got one gobbling that late and didn't kill him. Almost stepped on a five-foot rattle snake – you can believe I killed him.

Day 5 – chased same turkeys in lower woods out of hearing range

Day 6 – drizzling early, turkeys all gobbling off property, but they walked again all the way to Sci's property – got on them at 8:00, yelped, and never heard from them again

Day 7 – same pair gobbling and walking away in lower woods – it's becoming obvious that these are walking turkeys. Dad went back to the house and slept. I went to Sci's. Made the same pasture turkey gobble that I did on Day 4 (now appropriately named Snake), but now he was in the woods. He came up slowly, strutting and gobbling over 30 minutes – took him!

Day 8 – chased the walking turkeys all over the river side of the creek. Becoming more obvious – walking turkeys can't be killed. Sound like young mature gobblers. Walking turkeys always gobble a lot and always come in pairs. New theory is that they love to gobble but worry about getting beat up by bigger, older gobblers, so they stay away from hens so they can keep gobbling. That's why they're always moving.

Day 9 – set up close to the walking turkeys at roost, but they went other direction. Chased them, circled them, got in front of them, repeated the maneuver several times, and last heard them gobbling way off, likely a half-mile from where they roosted. The hell with walking turkeys. They can't be killed. Got another turkey to gobble at 8 o'clock – gobbled only twice in 2 ½ hours – didn't come close to killing him – Time to leave Cherokee Hollow.

Day 10 – Power Line Turkey at Shelby Co. gobbled ¾ of a mile from where we listened. Got on him, worked him a little, then he shut up. Power Line Turkey is becoming a famous character.

Miss 6 April 13, 2002 – Uwaharrie National Forest, North Carolina

Listened where I found turkeys a year before. Got there an hour and a half early so had to pass the time by sleeping in the truck (was worried about someone getting there before me). Listened down road and one gobbled early. Gobbled at every owl, and I was able to get close. Was in 15-year-old pine plantation next to cutover. I should have set up on the edge of the cutover, but didn't. Gobbled well and took him a long time to fly down. Then shut up. One started gobbling back by truck. Then mine gobbled again on the edge of the cutover and to my right. I spun. Silence for 10 minutes. Then all of a sudden saw him at 35 yards. He got behind some thick stuff, so I moved my gun. He halted for 30 seconds then started putting. He stepped out in an opening, but my gun still wasn't on him. He then went behind a tree, so I got my gun on him. He stepped out and started to trot away. Took a desperation shot. Don't think I even knocked him down. He flew away fast. Found where my shot pattern hit a tree near where he was. The center was nipple high, the bottom was above my waist and the top was at my neck. Didn't find a feather, blood, or messed up leaves. I shot over him. Will go back after him in two days.

Addendum – never heard him again

Miss 7 March 29, 2003 – Greene County (Cherokee Hollow)

Day one of our weeklong trip. We arrived late at the camp (midnight). Since it was raining and cold in the morning, Dad slept in while I couldn't stand it and went out. I listened in the lower woods by the middle creek. Despite intermittent light showers, there were moments of silence when I could have easily heard a gobble but didn't. Well, after it got light enough, a jake nearby started yelping and cutting and throwing in occasional rusty gobbles. I played with him, but he wouldn't come. After 15 minutes of this, a turkey way past him began gobbling and moving closer. The jake met up with him and as they started to move off, I saw three turkeys slightly to my right walking in at 100 yards. I spun, yelped, and one of them gobbled.

Two adult gobblers and one hen moved in slowly. Because they moved more to my right, I got the gun up left handed and waited for them to get close enough, all the while very worried they would see me in the open forest. The lead turkey gobbled three more times on his own and did some semi-strutting. Finally, he stepped out from behind a tree, stuck his head up, and seeing no reason to wait, I shot. I knocked him down, but he got up fast and flew away well. I can only hope he lived. I believe this is the fifth turkey I've missed with this gun and barrel (new Ithaca chambered for 3-inch shells). I will never use it again.

Kill 46 March 31, 2003 – Greene County (Cherokee Hollow)

Cold, windy, rainy weather characterized our first three days together on our week vacation; plus both Dad and I missed one, so it was becoming quite disconcerting. Sunday afternoon we met and looked at Mr. Trice's land over down in Gilbertown. It was unproductive, so Monday morning we came back to Cherokee Hollow. Driving in the main road, we saw two tremendous gobblers crossing the main field alone and heading from the bottom pines to the pines by the pond. We pulled down the road and into the pines 300 yards away and parked. We eased through the pines 100 yards, picked a couple of trees and called. In 10 minutes, I heard close drumming. Then he appeared very close. He got behind a tree, drummed again, and I got my gun up. He stepped out and I took him. Twenty-five pounds – what a turkey. Dad killed one later around 1 o'clock, greatly lifting our spirits

Kill 47 April 3, 2003 – Clay County

Halfway through our vacation, we left Cherokee Hollow to hunt Oak Hill (formerly LBV farm, now our farm) and Clay County. To our utter dismay, we heard absolutely nothing on our place in the morning. We left and by 9 o'clock were hunting around Mark's field. After hearing nothing below it, we walked halfway up the mountain road and made one gobble. He only gobbled a little and we never really got on him, but we were excited and went back the next morning. Early, while still dark, two started gobbling on the ridge directly above the field. We circled above at a fast pace and set up to the closest one on the side of the adjacent ridge. The closest was 200 yards away and two others were a couple hundred yards behind him. They were absolutely gobbling their heads off. Dad sat behind me, having forgotten his hearing protection. We both called, which they all aggressively responded to. While it was still relatively dark, too dark for any turkey in his right mind to fly down, I suddenly heard a close drum in front of me. I got ready and finally saw him about 35 yards in front. The farther two were still out there gobbling their heads off. He slowly came in, looking and semi-strutting, and I easily took him at 25 steps.

I left him to flop on his own while Dad joined me at my tree. We played with the other gobbling turkeys, in fact calling them pretty close (close enough to see), when they finally eased off. We chased them a long way and last heard them gobbling way off toward the mud road. They acted like a pair of walking turkeys with young gobbles – but there just may be a good ending – see kill # 48!

Kill 48 April 4, 2003 – Clay County

The sweetness of this one was remarkable. So many factors involved.

The day prior I killed one above Mark's field, and we heard at least five others around the area including the bowl near mud road. You can guess where we wanted to go the next morning. The trouble was, Andy and Tisdale (club members) both grabbed Mark's field and mud road before we got there to sign out. Tisdale had hunted WW ridge the day before and heard one far off which didn't interest him too much. Left with few options, and not knowing how to get to the turkey Tisdale heard up behind WW's house, we went there.

There were turkeys gobbling all over the place on the other side of the ridge, but most were off the property. About 7:30, we left, topped the ridge and heard one way off towards the intersection (Deer Head Road). We took off, walked a loooong way, and found they were across the road in the woods near that green field somewhat near the intersection. There were two and they were gobbling well. We crawled into the woods, finally found a place, and lightly called. They responded and within 10 minutes, I heard walking. Then I saw the first one while the other gobbled. They came in looking, semi-strutting and gobbling, slowly. This was our chance for a double. At one point after asking Dad if he was ready, I counted to three and pulled the trigger – but the safety was on and I flinched like you wouldn't believe. Thank God they didn't see me – which I can't understand why. But apparently Dad hadn't heard me correctly and wasn't ready to shoot. They walked a little closer, I counted to three again, and we shot. Mine went down good, but Dad's got up and ran to our left. I chased him and was catching up when I heard Dad yelling, "Shoot him, shoot him, shoot him." Finally, I had an open shot. He was about 30 yards, I remembered to pull the other trigger on the Fox Sterlingworth double, beaded his head, and shot. If I ain't a good wing shooter (hitting the head of a running turkey is actually harder than wing shooting) then I don't know who is. I nailed him.

Back in Goodwater, a log had been started to record when and where people hunt turkeys and the turkeys they killed. We entered both of ours for a recorded Henderson team total of three in four days. We had slipped in, worked the place over, and kicked ass!

We later found out that Tisdale heard nothing at Mark's field. He had to be sick at what he read when he returned.

Kill 49 April 19, 2003 – Shelby County

There just ain't nothing like digging one out.

We listened at the start of , where Dad had been working one earlier in the season, but heard nothing. So we trolled the Jade until I made one gobble not 75 yards away on the road in front of me. Maybe I spooked him going back to get Dad and maybe not, but for the next hour he never gobbled again. We found his strut marks at the intersection where the road peels off Jade to go down the mountain. So we decided to work that road to the bottom. It was covered in tracks.

Near the bottom, we made one gobble below us in the woods. Let me tell you that his was maybe the most awesome gobble I've ever heard. Sure the turkey had a good gobble, but something about that location imparted unique acoustics drawing it out and amplifying it. It tore me up inside.

For the next hour, he answered us frequently at a distance of 150 to 200 yards, but our set up was horrible and he just wouldn't come closer.

Then he gobbled and sounded to me like he had moved off and over a ridge. I moved us in fast – down, across the creek, and up almost to the top where he had to have previously been. We set up.

I yelped and he answered on top of us but behind and to the left – just on the other side of the crest of the hill. The tree was bad for spinning, so we swiftly scooted over to another tree: Dad facing the turkey with me on his right. Within a minute, I heard him drum; then walking that was moving to the right; then I saw him close and when he stood tall, I just couldn't stand it. I took him with the Ithaca 16-gauge. The turkey was supposed to be Dad's, but I got him instead. Dad was needing one bad after a dry spell. But he enjoyed every minute of it and as always, was so happy to see and be with his son to enjoy it together. It has been a real joy to hunt with Dad through the years. I can't hardly think of turkey hunting without him. I hope I don't have to for a long time!

Kill 50 March 20, 2004 – Greene County (Cherokee Hollow)

Well, since they've decided to open the season so early now, Dad and I decided to hunt the 19th and 20th at Cherokee Hollow – along the Black Warrior River where they gobble earlier in the season. River turkeys just gobble so much more and earlier in the season and earlier in the day than hill turkeys, and this trip was no exception. We headed back to the back part of the property on Day 1, parking the golf cart before it was really cracking. Just as we stepped out, one gobbled straight in the woods down from the twin field. Turned out to be three gobblers who loved to gobble. After the second and third turkeys would gobble at the first, the first would gobble back starting the series all over again. Conglomerations of gobbles would last sometimes 15 seconds before quitting. It turned out to be an extremely amusing hunt though we didn't kill any.

When they flew down, it sounded as if they were across that big creek at the bottom, so we ran back to the golf cart and went around to that high field bordering the creek on the other side to find them. They gobbled and we decided they really were on the other side where we started the morning – so we ran back around. Easing through the woods to set up, they gobbled, and it was now obvious they were in fact on the other side of the creek from where we now stood. So we ran around the bridge (foregoing the golf cart this time) and eased into the woods and worked them for 15 minutes. When they eased off, but still gobbling, we ran up closer to them and realized the creek curved left – and believe it or not, we decided they were on the other (original) side of the creek. So we ran around again, set up, and worked them for 15 minutes before they finally moved off somewhere and quit gobbling.

The next morning we got ready earlier, walked out the door at 4:50 and over to get the golf cart. After opening the door, Dad heard a turkey gobble in the pitch-black dark (not even thinking of cracking) down in the bottom woods below the house. So we abandoned the original operation of going back to twin field and headed down to the woods. Turned out the same three turkeys were down there and, again, they gobbled their heads off. Must have not had hens with them this time because they came in shortly after flying down. I took the lead turkey at 29 steps while one behind him at 35 steps was strutting his guts out.

Man, turkeys are gorgeous. Wonderful classic kill.

Kill 51 March 31, 2004– Shelby County

There ain't nothing like woods/hill country hunting. If you don't think it is harder than bottomland or field hunting, then you're a fool. Dad and I have been taking week-long trips exclusively for turkey hunting during the last part of March or first part of April for the past 10 years or so. During this week (really nine days considering both weekends on either side), we have always split our time between various places – Pickens County, Hale and Green Counties, Coosa and Clay Counties, and more recently, Shelby County. We discovered Shelby about seven years ago. Every turkey we heard gobble there for the first three or four years, we killed. They were easy. We didn't hunt there that much and didn't find all that many turkeys, but the ones that did gobble died an honorable death. Back then, the turkeys there did not have good, strong gobbles. You couldn't hear them very far away, and they lacked that thundering quality of other turkey gobbles.

Well, ladies and gentlemen, things have changed. All the turkeys in Shelby County are as real as real gets. Their gobbles have become awesome – and they've become impossible to kill.

Ten days in a row from March 27 to April 5 we hunted Shelby – and all of Shelby at that. Ten days and 13 gobbling turkeys of which we pulled the trigger on only three.

The day of Wednesday, March 31, was awesome and resulted in two of the three incidents alluded to above.

We discovered a new place we now call South of the Road across Highway 43 from the rest of the property (not to be confused with South of the Road in Clay Co.). Who would have ever guessed that while getting out of the truck while the sky was only barely cracking, a good 15 minutes before they had been gobbling the previous days, we would find one gobbling his head off across the highway. He sounded far, but reachable, and since it was so early and we had time to get to him, what more could we do but go? Little did we know.

We crossed the highway by the church, walked behind what we could only guess was the pastor's house, and headed up the mountain. Up and up we went and he'd gobble and damn if he wasn't still farther up. So up more and more and damn he was still farther up. By the time we finally approached his vicinity, we were nearly at the top of the giant mountain which only a fool would walk up.

We approached a half-rock cliff, scalable in places, and determined he was roosted lateral to us at about the same height as the cliff. We guessed he'd fly down on the top part, so we scaled it and set up.

He gobbled his head off and in 20 min, flew down – BELOW US! Not being able to see him, but being connected by sound (the way it should be), he circled below us to the other side and found a place to walk up the cliff to our level behind us. Fortunately, I realized this in time and spun. For the next hour, he stayed in two or three places drumming and gobbling, refusing to move forward even an inch. I sat in plain view of him (125 yards away) for at least half the time. Being on the edge of a steep mountain after spinning on a tree without the chance to prepare a seat left me in the most awkward of positions – and I stayed there for an hour!

Once he tried to leave and some light clucks stopped him. Finally, he folded and started coming. He dipped out of view. I got ready knowing that if he kept coming, he'd be in range the next time I saw him.

Then I saw dogs up the mountainside. Then I saw the turkey flying to my right in front of me. I beaded his head, had a marvelous shot, and decided the whole moment was far too grand to spoil on a wounded turkey should my aim not be perfect.

Was I mad the dogs came – yes. But I was left satisfied because the whole experience; walking nearly up the entire mountain side, sitting in an area that I was absolutely positive no one had ever set up and called to a gobbling turkey for a radius of half a mile, in beautiful woods, on a gorgeous morning, listening to the breathtaking sound of a genuine Alabama wild turkey gobble, in the woods, away from any fields was absolutely awesome.

Back down by the truck, we made another turkey gobble, called him up, and Dad killed him at 7:30.

Later on, up the road by gate 5, we made yet another turkey gobble that we had worked two days prior (and had spooked him), and called him up – and I killed him at 9:30.

Think I was glad I didn't shoot that first turkey on the wing?

MASTERING THE ART

Finally free of school and training, I returned to Alabama to resume my pursuit of hunting Alabama turkeys on a nearly full-time basis. For the next six years, Dad and I killed a lot of turkeys. The Greene and Shelby County properties remained extremely productive tracts. We continued making jaunts into Clay County and the Coosa County properties including Taliaferro Farm and LBV Farm (though we purchased and renamed it Oak Hill and later Montane) as well as discovering a neighbor's, Mr. Gilliland, properties (Cat Den and Golf Course). We spent minimal time going to a club in Camp Hill of Tallapoosa County where we killed two turkeys. Overall, these six years were the most successful to date. We were truly mastering the art of calling and killing gobbling wild turkeys.

Early in this stretch of stories, you'll read of an incident which led to a paradigm shift in our values for pursuing and shooting turkeys by committing to only hunt and kill gobbling turkeys that were legitimately called up. In the story, I detail how Dad shamefully killed a majestic, deep hardwoods gobbler that he did nothing to earn. In previous stories, you read about me ambushing two turkeys, both of which left me with an empty feeling. This one left Dad with a similar empty feeling. Both of us had killed many grand turkeys in glorious fashion over the years, such that we now realized the value in doing so the right way. Gobblers are too majestic to be ambushed or killed by dishonorable tactics, and we vowed to never do so again.

About this same time, while we were mastering the art of killing turkeys in honorable fashion, the state legalized the use of decoys which had the exact opposite effect on turkey hunting as a whole. Killing turkeys has since become commonplace. So many people hunt turkeys now, and they all too often kill turkeys by sitting on green fields with decoys out. The art we were mastering was being lost in the masses

You'll also see more moments of using vintage weaponry to shoot turkeys. I stumbled across an old stash of blue paper Peters #4 shells that I've since used on many occasions, often pairing it with the Fox Sterlingworth for a true throwback. And the L.C. Smith continued its long reign of success, never missing over its entire career, killing turkeys with vintage paper and plastic shells.

Kill 52 March 26, 2005 – Coosa County (Oak Hill)

Old Peters #6 – ain't nothing like that blue shell! And what a turkey! Woods hunting is just so classic. There really ain't no proper way to kill a turkey other than in the woods.

The farm has been just loaded this winter and early spring due to our conversion of pastures to native grasses. One day, we saw seven strutting around one area before they busted up. Could have easily shot one – but we didn't call him, so he still walks. Now they are scattered around the property.

Daybreak: two gobbling over in Mr. Gilliland's property and then one in the park. Dark enough to move closer, we set up just off the park and saw two strutting in trees as well as several other turkeys. Only one was gobbling. Then one behind us towards the loop started gobbling his head off. When the group in front of us flew down towards the field, we crossed over to the Chicken Coop road. He was gobbling down the road across the dam. So we crossed the hollow and up three-quarters of the ridge before I yelped and he gobbled on top the ridge. We hit two trees quickly.

He gobbled great and topped the ridge in view at about 75 yards – there he stayed and strutted and gobbled for 45 minutes. We got silent. He finally folded and eased down to, where at 34 steps, I took him.

I honor him.

Kill 53 April 7, 2005 – Shelby County

Well, in various aspects of life, one may find that he has accepted a higher standard of pursuit – in this case, the pursuit of turkeys. I've heard some proclaim before that they will let a turkey walk, and for the most part I chalked it up to less-than-noble interests and more to a lack of desire. But Dad and I let one walk earlier this season because we neither called him up nor heard him gobble. We just happened to sneak up on him on the edge of a field and we long ago decided we would never ambush a turkey again (see Kill 30, April 17, 1997). Now we've taken it to a higher level – a new level of purism.

It was a cloudy and potentially drizzly morning, though daybreak really wasn't all that bad. We tried to find the middle country turkey who had beat us for the past two years, but to no avail. Our trolling took us to the old original grounds before the power line down middle road (out of the middle country turkey's domain). One answered Dad's yelp far off down the ridge where they always are. We eased down 150 yards, set up, and the two-hour-and-forty-five-minute game began. He gobbled well, always courteous enough to gobble when he moved to let us know of his change in location. From 200 yards out to our left, he circled to 100 yards in front and sat there out of sight for 30 minutes. Then he circled closer to 75 yards to our right. At one point he must have been in range as his gobble was so loud, but we still never saw him. After a while he quickly left and went back to where he came from if not past it.

We jumped up, ran up the ridge and crossed over to the ridge he started on and eased down. He gobbled 200 yards off now in front of us. We yelped and he moved quickly back to where we had just come from – likely on top of the trees we were sitting at. There he gobbled at us for 30 minutes and slowly eased closer.

Finally, I saw him 80 yards off working in but angling down the ridge. A few light clucks and yelps turned him, and I beaded him until I took him at 28 steps. What an awesome turkey.

But the defining (and terrible) moment came 45 minutes later. While carrying the turkey out, and while talking in normal voices about various things like the dogwoods blooming, a turkey gobbled in front of us just around a slight roll in the terrain, likely within gun range. Not positive we really heard a gobble (since real turkeys just don't do this sort of thing when you are announcing to the woods your presence with normal talking), we immediately hit two trees with Dad in front. He gobbled again. We squirmed and got comfortable. Dad yelped and not five seconds later, he slipped out to our right 15 steps away. Dad turned his gun, and I whispered as loud as I felt comfortable, "don't shoot." All Dad heard was "shoot," and he killed him though he really didn't want to. The whole affair lasted perhaps 45 seconds. We were sick and made a vow to never kill a turkey again if we didn't truly earn him. We hadn't earned this turkey, we just got lucky.

Kill 54 April 21, 2005 – Shelby County

Good grief. They all shut down for the past two weeks. After the last kill, for a day or two, we found lots of turkeys and even called a couple up, but no shot. But then they all stopped gobbling. All in Shelby just completely shut down. We've been trying so hard to get one to gobble, only successful every now and then. I have heard so few gobble on roost this year. It is getting very old.

Dad had made one gobble south of the road one mid-morning about a week before the above date, but probably spooked him getting close. The next day, we found him gobbling on roost, but he shut up. However, we did happen to see him come by at about 50 or 60 yards following some hens strutting. I watched him for an hour on another ridge strutting (and mating twice!). He never did gobble again.

The morning at hand, I listened in the same spot – nothing. I worked his area – nothing. I then worked across the lower portion of south of the road finally crossing the road that goes up to the mountain. I found fresh strut marks at that intersection just before the ascent. About 100 yards down the bottom road that cuts south, he gobbled (same or different turkey??) 150 yards away to the right. I found a good tree, called, and had a delightful exchange. He was courteous and gobbled at everything. Then, after about 15 minutes, he came, weaving down one of the motorcycle paths until I took him at 25 steps with the Fox Sterlingworth and an old paper Peter's #4.

Dad heard the boom far off from the Jade Fox. He wondered if it was me. It was!

Kill 55 March 29, 2006– Shelby County

The gobbling wasn't great starting out this year. Of course, turkey season now starts March 15, and I, like an idiot, have been almost every day since it opened. Nothing is greening out yet. Neither Dad nor I have heard much gobbling up to today.

We started the day on Jade Fox where we had seen a tremendous gobbler strutting once and lots of tracks. He has yet to gobble. I think we even spooked him as we walked out of there. We worked middle road to no-name area. Before the big rocks, we parked and eased down to the right behind the rocks to yelp. We have done this so many times before, and so many times have made one gobble. Today was no different.

He gobbled down in there to the left pretty far. We walked only a short way before we got nervous because the leaves weren't out. We set up at two different trees. He gobbled again, then silence. Finally he gobbled again more directly below us – he was moving to the right. He kept moving to the right so that we had to spin on the tree. He seemed to get close, but a giant boulder was blocking our view. I finally heard walking and saw him about 60 yards out easing up the ridge, now 180 degrees from where he started. There were two turkeys. He kept gobbling periodically, but not too much. We only called lightly. I lost eyesight. He dallied out there from 75 to 150 yards moving about, gobbling occasionally. I finally saw him again once, walking away. His gobbles got more faint. They finally got so far that we jumped up and walked down 20 yards to get away from the boulder. We considered chasing him, but decided to wait him out. We each found great seats at two big longleafs.

Shortly after sitting down again, he gobbled fairly close, and almost above us. Then he gobbled far off again. He seemed to be moving around so much. Then I heard walking above me, then a gobble, and down the rocks comes a gobbler with a hen. I was holding the gun left handed. He stopped and I pulled the trigger, but the safety was on. He was already suspicious and beginning to spook. He turned and started to walk away. I fumbled with the safety trying to unlock it with my left hand and finally did so – just in time. I took an almost desperation shot at about 30 yards. He went down. Now, I own him.

Kill 56 April 13, 2006 – Shelby County

I'm writing this in hindsight as the season is ending. It was perhaps the most uninspiring turkey season I've ever had. They just didn't gobble this year. We worked some. Had one gobbling good one day in the back cable area of Clay County, worked one several times near Mark's Field (he was always going away though), Dad killed one gobbling decent later in the morning on Jade Fox, and a few others here and there. But all and all, it was just a crappy year. This day, however, was awesome

We listened on the Jade where we always do. Dad thought he heard one way down towards Gate 5 road. We worked down real slow, and never seemed to get closer. We got way, way down and finally eased up that big hill. He was at the top but left and down the ridge a little bit. Near the top, we eased into the woods to the right and up the ridge a little. He gobbled pretty good and spent the first 20 minutes going away from us, further down the road. We considered moving, but stayed put. Then he slowly came in, always gobbling to let us know where he was. He showed straight in front of me about 60 yards where he stopped and stared for a while. Then he worked in. He started to get so close that, with the Fox Sterling-worth in hand, I switched my finger from the full choke trigger to the modified one. Finally, he stopped about 17 steps and I pulled the trigger with an old Peter's blue paper shell #4. He went down, but not well, im-mediately got up and flew a few feet off the ground to the left and landed no further than 20 feet from where he started. He ran a few steps and stopped in plain sight. I put the bead on his neck and fired the full choke, again with a paper blue Peter's. I got him good this time. It was absolutely beautiful there and it was a wonderful experience for father and son who were craving some good gobbling.

[I did not include this as a miss in the data section. The first shot didn't fire correctly. It wasn't loud and though the turkey went down, he didn't run or fly away at lightning speed. I felt at the time it must have been a defective paper shell.]

Kill 57 March 30, 2007 – Shelby County

What an amazing opening two weeks of season. A few years back, the state of Alabama moved opening day up five days to March 15, which was an idiotic move. This year, however, it opened with temps in the 80s. It continued with beautiful weather for almost three weeks before get-ting cold. So, while the first week is usually silent and boring, the turkeys opened the season gobbling well this year. Problem was, I didn't schedule any time off work during week one. I hunted the weekends, but went only twice over a week and a half.

Dad and I found one the week before at 10 o'clock working the mountain road on Gate 9. He gobbled down the mountain near the bottom one time only. The next morning, he gobbled well in the same spot, but took off on a journey towards the power line after he flew down. I went after him again a few days later, found him gobbling in the same area and got on him close while still pretty dark – which never works, and didn't work this time. He gobbled only once after flying down and seemed to be going away. After a while, I eased down to the bottom of the mountain and set up. After another short while, I heard a turkey walking up which turned out to be a hen. But, then I heard drumming and he came up following her. He went by me at 75 yards and out of sight. I eased back to the power line and saw him way down slipping across. Then another started gobbling behind him, and then he started gobbling a little bit too. I worked them for another hour before giving up and leaving.

A few days later, I entered the woods while dark from the power line. He gobbled near where he had been but up the mountain a bit. I eased up fairly close and found a comfortable longleaf to sit at. I was aiming diagonal up hill. He gobbled great and answered every call. While still fairly dark, he flew down and came right in, gobbling the whole way.

It has been a while since I hunted a turkey like this over the span of multiple mornings. I had gotten to know and respect him. Now I own him!

Kill 58 April 29, 2007 – Coosa County (Golf Course)

Well, this season the turkeys finally gobbled well for the first time in two and a half years. We got into good gobbling the first half of the season at Shelby and the last half of the season at Clay County. I killed two turkeys this season, but should have killed four (missed one and didn't pull the trigger on one I should have), called up two others within 20 steps behind me, and snuck up on a gobbler in Gilliland's pasture that I beaded and could have easily shot. All and all, I had a lot of fun, heard a lot of gobbling, worked many off roost, called a lot in, but just didn't kill many. That's okay. I had two turkeys this year that I hunted on multiple days, one being dead and the other was the one I should have pulled the trigger on. He was walking in at 20 steps, my bead was on him, but there were some limbs in the way – I was going to let him walk past a tree and step out the other side when he saw Dad behind me and spooked. He spooked at 16 steps from me. I never had a decent shot as he trotted away. I hunted him several other times, the last when I got in great position on him and Andy ran me off. I won't get into that. [Andy was a club member at Clay County for whom countless stories could be told. In this case, we both approached a gobbling turkey from different directions that was right in the middle of our respective signed out locations, and when he saw me easing through the woods, he got angry. We later made amends.]

After all the work we did at the farm to attract turkeys, it was a bust. All the turkeys were off our property. Today was my last day to hunt turkeys, and once again, at the farm, the turkeys were off the property. After striking out, we went behind the golf course and made one gobble shortly after walking in. We slipped down a ridge and set up. It was beautiful. He gobbled well, answering our yelps and clucks. Then silence. After a while I heard walking, then saw him, then another. It was two – they worked in a little more. I followed the lead, though the one trailing clearly was the gobbling one. The trailing one stopped in an open spot looking for me. I think he saw me because I had to keep moving my gun to follow the lead gobbler. The lead gobbler stopped behind a tree twice, so I couldn't shoot. I knew he was kind of far. The back turkey started lightly putting. Finally, my turkey stepped out to the side. The shot wasn't great, and it seemed far, but I couldn't let another one go. My shot knocked him down well, but when I got to him, he seemed to gain some strength and half run/flop away. I dove on him. He ripped my pants to shreds. I now own him. Thank you, God for another!

Kill 59 March 28, 2008– Shelby County

Mystic Mountain has become a hot spot. With the longleaf pines that smatter its hillside, it is awesome.

Like last year, I got on one for several days in a row. We first saw him one day way down the power line. He was with hens, so we left him. Later that day, we made him gobble in the woods once, but nothing more happened. The next day was Easter. We were eating an 8:00 snack on the edge of the power line. He eased up about 80 yards away catching us unaware. The next day I went after him at the crack of dawn from the hill way down the power line. Sure enough, he gobbled on Mystic Mountain. I chased him around until I had to leave and he shut up. The next day, I again went after him from the power line. But like the day before, he seemed to stay on top. I eventually ran into him on the mountain road. He was strutting before I spooked him away. The next morning, I was on top the mountain by the road, but he stayed at the bottom. I never even got close to working him before he shut up. Then, the next morning (the day at hand), I went after him again from the bottom. And once again, he was up top and stayed up there. I slowly eased his direction figuring he was on the road again. I eased up to the same spot I saw him strutting two days before, this time more cautious so as not to spook him if he was there. And he was there, strutting his guts out. I sat at a tree, yelped lightly, and in a few minutes he was in front of me.

The Mystic Mountain turkey is no more. I'm sure another will come to replace him.

Miss 8 2008 – Coosa County (Taliaferro Farm)

We found one gobbling early at the farm and set up close. He flew down while very dark, and appeared in front of me, having walked up a logging skidder run. He was close. I took a quick shot; didn't even knock him down. I'm sure he lived.

Kill 60 March 30, 2008– Shelby County

I'll do my best with this one, because it was one of the coolest kills, but so full of mystique that it is hard to describe:

It was a crappy day – wet from rain overnight, cloudy, foggy, and windy. And where did we go? – to a power line on the top of the mountain. A power line that funnels wind and a mountaintop that can be windy on the most calm of days. A couple of times while listening, I thought my hat was going to blow off. To no surprise, we heard nothing but the howling wind, so we eased past the power line. We'd run into Danny (properties manager) there the day before. He had taken several clients turkey hunting. He said they heard four or five turkeys gobbling past the power line, both on the right and left sides of the road. So needless to say, we were eager to see for ourselves.

We eased down the road and then up to the ridge top to listen on both sides. We sat and yelped a little and realized that we were being ridiculous. No turkey in his right mind was going to even think of gobbling in this kind of weather.

So we eased back down to the road to leave. On the way out, a turkey gobbled at one of my owls. He was across the road, pretty far in the woods and in the direction of the power line. We eased in and set up pretty far away. We've always wanted to work a turkey on that side of the road. It is awesomely beautiful. And while clouds, wind and fog normally make beautiful woods atrocious in the eyes of a turkey hunter, these woods felt magical. The leaves were just starting to come out with their light greens speckling the woods. The chestnut oaks were painted in mossy green lichen. And the forest floor was turning green from that blueberry-like plant that covers that area. Coupling these light greens and back drop of rain-soaked bark and darkened forest floor with the muting of the canvas by the fog, it was almost as if we were working a turkey in a dream. It was awesome.

After five or ten minutes, he finally gobbled again, but sounded farther away. So we moved down the semi-ridge towards him. The fog helped us feel hidden. We didn't really go that far before we set up again. We called and sat in silence for another 15 minutes or so. Finally, Dad got to working his slate. Suddenly, he gobbled to our left, close and just up another semi-ridge. I spun as best I could. In a few minutes, down came two gobblers closing fast. They got close and I shot the lead one. The other jumped a few steps and stopped. Dad, who was sitting behind me, shot him too.

It was a double in an enchanted woods on the most unlikely of days. Doubt I'll ever do that again.

Kill 61 April 3, 2008 – Shelby County

This one was quick. I listened at the second listening spot when walking from the top of Jade Fox. He gobbled down towards the first listening spot. I ran down the road and he gobbled down on the other side of the mountain. I eased over, and found he was much closer than expected. I set up, called some, and he gobbled some. Shortly, he flew down, gobbled twice a little to the right, and came in. It was as simple as that.

Kill 62 April 4, 2008 – Shelby County

What a week. Today is Friday. Last Friday, I killed my first of the season. Now I own four. And this one was awesome.

With the threat of bad weather, Dad and I parked inside Gate 2 and headed across to the tip of Easter Mountain. [Dad had killed two turkeys on successive Easter mornings on this mountain ridge – thus the name, Easter Mountain] We had heard one gobbling his head off there Easter morning. Dad also worked him there the next day. This day, however, was cloudy, causing him to gobble 20 minutes later than the past mornings. He was past the tip of Easter Mountain and up on the steep mountainside where Gate 1 Road runs.

We eased around the mountain tip, crossed the creek and up the mountainside a bit. Dad wanted to go up a road to the intersection and then follow the road towards the turkey so we would be even level with him. Knowing how steep the side of the mountain where the turkey was, I convinced him to stay near the bottom. We found an awesome knoll at the base, so I could see the side real well. He gobbled great. We called only a little. After a while, silence – which always means – He then gobbled fairly close, and I saw him easing down the mountain. It took another 20 minutes from there. He found a couple of places to set up and strut and gobble. We watched the whole thing and it was awesome. Finally, he folded and got close enough for me to feel comfortable with the Fox Sterlingworth and an old Winchester paper shell #6 inside. Boooooommmm. What an awesome classic kill.

Kill 63 April 11, 2008 – Shelby County

We started the morning on the hillside of the Gate 5 road. Dad had seen some strut marks there the day before and got fired up. Indeed, I had worked two on opening morning there for three hours gobbling their heads off.

The day cracked with spotty rain. We heard nothing anywhere, any direction. Finally, we worked Jade Fox. Dad again got fired up over strut marks found down the entire road. But we heard nothing. At the top of Jade, we made one gobble down near the old green field. He gobbled good right up to the point when we started calling. I don't think we spooked him, but something sure happened.

So we worked Turkey Valley towards the power line – like we've done a billion times – a task that is usually futile. But today it wasn't.

He gobbled just past the swamp – just after Dad and I discussed how we had never heard a turkey gobble around there. He gobbled down at the bottom, if not the other side of Turkey Valley. We parked and moved down the ridge before easing into the valley a little way. The turkey answered everything, though we didn't call much. He came right on but not too quickly. I saw his fan about 100 yards out. He looked good coming in the beautiful chestnut oak-dominated open, mature forest. I busted him with an old paper shell #6 in the L.C. Smith 16-gauge. God is good for his creation. Thank you, God for letting me experience your awesomeness.

Kill 64 April 2, 2009 – Shelby County

What a turkey. I hunted him four different days. And he was something. The first day of season, on a crummy, drizzly morning, we heard him gobble once across the power line and down near that old chimney. A week or two later, he gobbled again in the same general location. We set up close to him and saw him fly down, but he moved down the hill away from us. The next time, I got on him early in the dark at the beginning of a thunderstorm. I had walked down the power line in the dark, eased in the woods, and he gobbled close. I flushed a hen on top of me and later four others roosting around me too. He gobbled his head off at far away thunder, my yelps, my clucks, owls, and any noise there was. Because of the approaching storm, it stayed dark until almost seven o'clock when I saw him fly down my direction. I figured I had him. But, again, he moved off.

So the next day we went at him from the top. He was in the same general area again. Once again, it started drizzling on us. He started gobbling on roost and never stopped for three hours and 50 minutes. He moved around in front of us a bit, between 100 and 300 yards out. We only moved once. But he finally came in. It was drizzly and foggy like last year, giving it a mystical quality.

It was awesome. Dad sat behind me and enjoyed the whole thing.

Afterwards, we knelt and gave the whole experience to God. Praise our Almighty!

Kill 65 April 3, 2009 – Tallapoosa County (Camp Hill)

This may have been the quickest I've ever killed. Early that morning, we went to Clay County – to the big green field where we found one gobbling. We circled that knoll on the corner and sat on the other side of it, halfway up the knoll. I saw him just after sitting. He proceeded to gobble at everything for 30 minutes, then folded and marched in. Dad was the shooter. He was shooting the Ithaca 16-gauge. which he missed a turkey with several years ago. So he was nervous. He let the turkey get real close and then shot. He missed, spent his last three shells in desperation and I chased the turkey out into the field. He flew off. Though Dad knocked him down, we found a 1 ½-inch tree three steps in front of him shot in half. Apparently the tree took out his pattern. So we left, hopeful that the turkey would live.

We headed to scout Camp Hill and parked at the gate. We walked in and were told the camp house was a short walk. We quickly came to the small lake with a shed by the road. Just past it, I yelped and one gobbled real close in the direction of the house. We backed up in the woods, yelped again and he gobbled closer. He then appeared, strutted briefly twice and worked into the woods to my left. I took him with the Fox Sterlingworth. Though it was quick, it was awesome. I'll take it.

We think he was in the green field in front of the house when he first gobbled.

Kill 66 April 9, 2009 – Shelby County

Boom – got him, but it was all just a terrible mistake. I eased in the woods below the landing while dark. Dad and I had found one there a week earlier. He answered my owl, close, while dark. I sat down and he gobbled good. Then another gobbled fairly close somewhere behind me, across the road. I heard a turkey fly down though I wasn't sure which one. Then I heard walking – but it was coming up to my left. Finally, I turned my head way left and a mature gobbler was walking up from behind perhaps 15 yards away. It was pretty dark. He sensed me and got nervous. He kept walking, though cautiously and angling away. I was in a dilemma as whether or not to move my gun around a tree and commit to him, though I risked spooking him doing so, and if I did move my gun around and the other walked up in front of me, then I'd be in trouble. Well, I tried anyway, barely got the gun around, but never got a good shot and I sure didn't want to miss.

After he walked out of sight, the turkey in front gobbled again sounding as if he had walked off and was on the landing. So I got up and circled around to the bottom of the road that shoots off the landing. I sat on a knoll facing the landing and yelped a few times. In a few minutes I heard walking to my left – where I had come from. Then I saw a gobbler working down the opposite ridge coming towards me. I figured it was the gobbler that came up behind me, and I wasn't about to let him get away again. He had a mature head and looked good coming. I spun and took him at 18 steps – a jake. Like I said – it was all just a terrible mistake. But he sure tasted good at Easter lunch.

Kill 67 April 26, 2009 – Shelby County

Shelby County turkeys are a different breed than those around Hatchet Creek. We spent the latter part of the season hunting the farm and Joe Gilliland's property. They have been gobbling like crazy there, especially in the Cat Den. But like Hatchet Creek turkeys have always been (formerly known as Lanny Vines turkeys), they are just impossible to call in. [I'm referring once again to the difficult Coosa County turkeys found at the properties close to Hatchet Creek. To this day they are still the most difficult turkeys to call up compared to turkeys in all the other locations we hunted through the years.] But this year they've gobbled good and acted a little better by answering our calls and not immediately running away, which was a lot of fun. Dad missed a great one in the Cat Den that was tough to swallow, but he lived and gobbled again another day.

After so much time with Hatchet Creek turkeys, I took a day and went back to Shelby County. Being alone, I decided to hunt Slide Mountain (back side of Chamber). Instead of walking up Slide Mountain, I listened on a knoll just off the Gate 6 road so I could hear the entire area. I got there while dark and heard a poacher working up in the woods. After running him off, I left, drove down the road towards Gate 7, and found a turkey gobbling across the Gate 7 road, perhaps by the power line. I set up across a creek and yelped. He immediately answered and then got silent for five minutes. Finally, I yelped again and he gobbled close having moved a little left. I got ready. Then he appeared down by the creek at 50 yards. He moved in moderately fast, stopping to strut a couple of times. He walked in close behind a bunch of small trees. I never got a shot until he was close.

As I said, Shelby County turkeys are a different breed. They come in so much easier than Hatchet Creek turkeys in Coosa County. I wonder if I'll ever be successful with a Hatchet turkey?

Kill 68 April 27, 2009 – Coosa County (Cat Den)

Well, in answer to the question in the last sentence of my previous kill story, YES!!! Finally! After so much work. I got him. I own him. And what a set of spurs.

We listened on the power line. They started gobbling everywhere. None were super close which left us running around trying to figure out which turkey to go after. We finally headed down the ridge to the left of the power line as one was gobbling down near the bottom but on Bobbit's side. When we set up, he quit gobbling. Don't know if we spooked him, but after a short time one started gobbling deep in the Cat Den where we had worked one many times this year. We had nicknamed him "Jake Man" because twice we called him in close, but he had jakes with him mucked up the situation.

So we went after him again, crossing the death-defying valley and up to the Cat Den road. We worked down it and found him gobbling almost as far as the back end. We set up by the road at the beginning of the transition to old growth hardwoods. It was beautiful and a good spot. Only problem was if the turkey came up the road, he would be fairly close before we saw him.

As is usual with Hatchet Creek turkeys, once we set up and called, he stopped gobbling good and never seemed interested in us. Finally, after 30 minutes, Dad got interested in going after a turkey gobbling behind us, way back up towards the front of the Cat Den. So he got up and left and

I hung with the turkey. I was itching to move forward to a spot where I could see better down the road. I once got up and walked a little forward, but didn't see any better trees, so I went back. Finally, after the turkey gobbled again and seemed to be even farther away, I got up again and walked farther down the road (but in the woods). I walked perhaps 30 yards. I still didn't find a good tree on my side, but I noticed a good tree on the other side of the road. I didn't want to cut across the road being that you could see pretty far down it. So I worked back to my original tree and planned to cross the road there. Just before turning to go across the road, I looked back down the road and saw a turkey walking down it. Then it stopped and strutted. It was him! He was perhaps 100 yards away. As he walked down to the bottom of the road, I dipped down out of view, slid up to my original tree and got ready. He finally appeared, moved in, strutted once, and I took him. Took him with an old blue original Peters shell! Dad ran back in amazement and kicking himself for leaving.

What a season. Limit again! God is good. Dad is too. Had great discussions with Dad this year about God. Great discussions and great prayer. Praise Him for He is worthy!

Kill 69 March 20, 2010 – Shelby County

A new year. I started opening day in Gate 6 and found two gobbling near the waterfall at the base of Slide Mountain. I eventually chased the turkey up Slide Mountain and pulled him in at 20 yards. But he saw me and spooked. Three days later, I found turkeys gobbling all over Slide Mountain. I even saw two gobblers, one on roost strutting, but couldn't draw them close enough. So the next time I went, I started on Slide Mountain where all the turkeys had been. As expected, one gobbled down the mountain and was a fast walking-away turkey. I last heard a faint gobble as he crossed from Shelby to Talladega County and eventually crossed the state line.

So having climbed the mountain before daybreak, and having run down the mountain chasing one, I decide to head back up Slide Mountain to the back end of the chamber. As I crested the chamber, I caught my breath and yelped. One hit it immediately in the chamber about 150 yards. I jumped to a tree, made a nice seat, put in my ears, got my head net and gloves on, and then got quiet. Soon as I got quiet, I heard walking. Then he appeared – marching slightly to my left. He came fast, less than five minutes from my initial yelp. I took him as he stopped for a brief look. WOW. The season has begun!

Miss 9 2010 – Clay County

We started on Willie Wilson's ridge and heard one way down the other side. It took us a while to get on him, but once we did, he worked and came in slowly. We were in wide open hardwoods staring uphill. Dad was filming. When the turkey came in, he stood tall acting as though he saw us. I'm sure he did. The shot was long and I had an old Paper Peter's shell in the Fox Sterlingworth. Not the most powerful of weapons. I don't even think I knocked him down. Agony. [I marked off the shot at 45 to 50 steps. I should have let him walk.]

Later that morning, we worked a turkey elsewhere for three and a half hours. He gobbled at everything the whole time. We finally left him in disgust.

Kill 70 March 26, 2010 – Shelby County

It is turning into the year of the quick kills. My first happened within five minutes of making him gobble. Later in the year, Dad (on Easter morning), killed one when it was so dark we could barely see the turkey. This turkey was quick too, he didn't even gobble, but it was awesome.

I had worked Shelby over pretty well this morning. I was alone and had little interaction with gobbling turkeys. But it was a gorgeous day. The leaves were just starting to come out, but the dogwoods weren't blooming yet. It had been a long, wet, and cold winter. The turkeys were definitely starting later than usual.

I parked below the landing and eased up a small rise not 50 yards from the truck. I yelped and a hen deep in the area answered me. I eased another 15 yards closer and set up looking down a beautiful shallow ridge. I yelped and she answered again 100 yards in front of me. I got my gloves, ears, and head net on. When I got set, I saw movement 75 yards in front of me. It stepped into an opening and was a beautiful, lit-up mature gobbler. The hen yelped behind him. He marched towards me to the top of the finger ridge jutting out from my seat. He was 35 yards. There, in the mosaic of sun and shade, among the smattering of delicate tree leaves and orderly hickory/oak tree trunks, he began to strut. I sat in silence, bead wavering around his head and body.

He walked five steps closer, strutted again, and stepped closer again. Dad and I had set a rule that we would never shoot a turkey that didn't gobble. I couldn't resist, and am glad I didn't. I had pulled a mature gobbler away from a hen, watched him strut in a beautiful wood, on a beautiful day, and had him at 25 steps. It was awesome. Thank you God!

Kill 71 March 27, 2010 – Shelby County

A day with my son Tripp. He is now five going on six. We started at the top of the power line, but heard nothing. So we started to road hunt on the way out. Past the big rocks, at perhaps the most successful spot for road hunting on the entire property, I made one gobble. [Road hunting was a technique Dad had perfected long ago in the National Forest, though I'm sure it's not so secretive now. We'd drive the dirt roads stopping period-ically to yelp down in the adjacent woods. If one gobbled, we'd go after him. If not, we'd drive on a little further. Road hunting allowed us to cover great distances later in a morning to find a gobbling turkey.] He was down in the old original area. I grabbed Tripp and set up down amongst the big boulders facing down the ridge. The turkey answered 200 yards away. He answered almost everything. Tripp was to my right, resting his head on my right shoulder. The turkey came and presented himself at 60 yards. There he strutted and gobbled for 10 minutes. While I saw all, Tripp's view was blocked by a boulder in front. At one point the turkey started to go away. But I turned him back. He eventually folded, marched in, and I took him with the L.C. Smith 16 and an old plastic Western Super X shell, and Tripp at my side.

Tripp never did see him, but he heard him and enjoyed every minute – except for the fact that he may have gotten tired for a minute. While watching the turkey strut, Tripp yawned, out loud, and the turkey gobbled back. Perhaps that is what pulled the turkey in. We could market it – the new yawn call.

Kill 72 April 9, 2010 – Tallapoosa County (Camp Hill)

New areas are so sweet. While exploring Camp Hill, we made a turkey gobble down a road past a green field. It was 11:00. We worked him for the next hour and a half, moving slightly closer three separate times. Finally, at the last position, after a period of silence, he gobbled close and moved more to my right. Dad was filming behind me. I heard him walking, and saw him coming slowly at about 75 yards. He worked in and I took him with the Ithaca 16-gauge. Dad barely got him on film before I shot.

Despite the brevity of the above story, the kill was awesome. My best of the year. It was classic, middle of the day, beautiful weather, in an unknown territory, and he gobbled well for one and a half hours. Ahhhhhhh-hhhhh.

Kill 73 April 30, 2010 – Coosa County (Oak Hill)

Despite having killed four turkeys for the season, missed one, and watched Dad kill two, it turned out to be a tough season – especially the second half.

Shelby County shut down the second half as it always does. Doesn't make any sense. The turkeys are there, but they just won't gobble the second half of any turkey season – ever.

The Cat Den and Oak Hill were more typical than ever. We found many turkeys, made many of them gobble, but they always stop gobbling as you approach them. One day Dad heard six or seven gobbling for hours around the cabin. The next day we found only one. The mystery of turkey hunting.

As season drew to an end, we focused on the loop and Cat Den, occasionally finding them but nothing close to being successful. This last day of the season, we started behind the lake on the loop. We worked one off roost towards Willie's pasture, but he moved off fairly quickly. So we left and walked the loop past the sourwood savannah. As we headed up to the old house site, a hen answered us deep in the loop towards the chicken coop. As we walked on, and we yelped back and forth, a turkey gobbled opposite from her on the back loop road. We set up just off the middle loop road, facing the road with the turkey on the other side. He answered four or five times in a matter of five minutes. Then he came. I heard him walking and turned way left to meet him stepping out onto the road. There he quickly strutted and moved down the road towards us. I followed him with my L.C. Smith, beading him as he came. He got close, and I took him with an old plastic Western Super X #6. I now I own him. It was awesome. Thanks, Dad, for buying this place!

A SEASONED VETERAN

Turkeys don't gobble as much as they used to, and these next stories highlight such woes with fewer kills and frustrations written into the stories. Six years ago, I began participating in a state-sponsored survey, recording details of every hunt I go on for the entire turkey season to include how many different turkeys I heard gobble and how many gobbles I heard each day. The numbers of gobbles are estimates, of course, for who would ever keep an accurate tally of gobbles heard over the course of three hours when working the woods? But despite entering the data from memory at the end of the day and sometimes forgetting to do the task until the next day or a week later, the first four years (less a year I skipped) showed remarkable consistency in gobbles heard for the season (see Chart 8). The past two years, however, the gobbles heard were roughly half that of the previous four years. That's remarkable. Despite the lack of gobbling turkeys we found last year, we had some great hunts. In fact, March 31, 2018 (Kill 85) was perhaps the best day of turkey hunting I can remember. It also highlights the recurring theme of missing turkeys that has plagued my career.

Gobbles Per 10 Hours Hunted

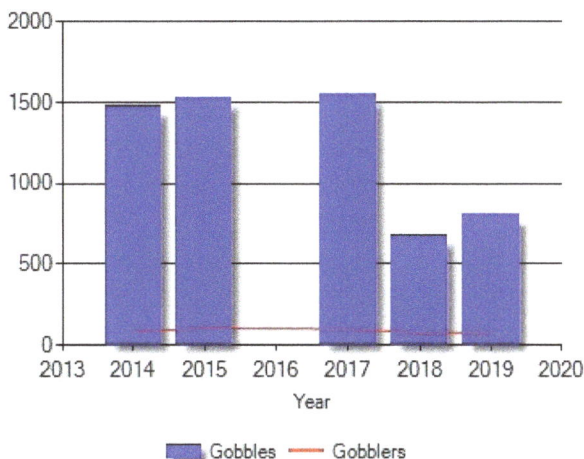

The Greene County bottomland tract has remained a staple location, seemingly never going south or breeding this new variety of shut-mouth gobblers. In contrast, Shelby County's turkey population declined to a point where we gave up on it several years ago. Same with Clay County. We continued to hunt Coosa County hard including our place (Montane) and our neighbor's (Cat Den and Golf Course) and had a three-year stretch in a new location (Hatchet Valley) that was awesome with deep hardwoods, longleaf savannahs and pine plantations. Aside from Hatchet Valley, the turkeys in Coosa County remain the most difficult to kill of any place we've ever hunted. If you tally up and compare the turkeys shot in all locations over the course of my hunting career, you'd think we had hunted the Coosa properties much less, but the exact opposite is true. We've spent more time chasing turkeys around our land and our neighbor's property than any other. For some reason, they are nearly impossible to call up.

The stories below introduce a brief stint into another new area, the Hollins Management Area in the Talladega National Forest. It is fairly close to our property, and we found many turkeys gobbling there the first two weeks of the first year we hunted it. Then they all shut up. Despite all the turkeys we found during that two-week stretch, they were public turkeys and nearly as difficult to call up as our place. But I did call up a pair and – well, I'll let you read about that below.

As we close out the stories, one ever-present theme percolates all right up to the end — the sustained and loyal companionship with my father. In the back cover blurb of my book, The Fire Tower, Tom Kelly writes, turkey hunting "is the most solitary of sports...." The point is well founded and a position I've held strong for a long time, but it's a position of foolery. For every hunt I've ever been on, Dad has been right there with me either physically or in spirit. When hunting together, we think and move through the woods as a single unit, sharing a bond forged with a single-minded purpose in the primeval forest. And if I'm hunting alone, who do you think I call immediately after, or these days, text, during or after the hunt? Recounting the events of both successful and unsuccessful hunts with such a friend is integral and necessary to the enjoyment of my pursuit. I like to say I hunt turkeys for the unique challenge it offers. But if I can't share the experience with someone who understands the meaning behind the details, then I fear this pursuit will lose its significance. And it's a true fear, because

I honestly wonder what I'll do when Dad departs. Not to get too morbid, but it will happen some day, hopefully no time soon, but he is 77 now. When it happens, will I keep turkey hunting? I hope and expect so, but I also fear the loss of such a close companion who has been an integral part of my hunting will take away such a vital part of my hunting enjoyment. For now, he is still with us and I relish the coming season, the turkeys I'll work, and sharing it all with my great friend and father. Enjoy!

Kill 74 March 2011 – Greene County (Cherokee Hollow)

I'm writing this a year later…

Can't believe I didn't write my story in a timely manner as I've done for 20 years.

Dad and I spent a few days at Cherokee Hollow in late March. We got into a lot of gobbling. One mid-morning, a day after Dad killed one in the bottom section, I left Dad, who was fishing, to go to Twin Fields. As I crossed the bridge, I yelped and one gobbled way up by the green field. I cut straight through the bottom woods to the field, that section we've always wanted to see a turkey walk through. As I approached the rise that feeds off the back of the field, he gobbled up in the field. I set up. He gobbled a few more times. I then heard drumming and saw him easing down the rise. Didn't take more than 15 minutes from the first gobble. But I took him, a great way to start the season.

Kill 75 April 2011 – Coosa County (Golf Course)

I'm writing this a year later…

I only killed two for the 2011 season. It was a tough season. They just didn't gobble well for the first two-thirds of the season. Dad killed one early at Cherokee Hollow and one late at Montane. In between, we spent a good bit of our time chasing gobbling turkeys around the cutover behind the golf course, and around the golf course itself. Every time we went to the Cat Den, we'd make one gobble across the road in the cutover or golf course. On this morning, that is just what we did. And we went over only to find they were moving away. Every time we'd get closer to their gobbling, they'd move away. After a while, easing back between the course and cutover, we heard a gobble way out in the cutover. We slipped up to a big tree on the edge and saw two strutting across on a ridge top. They gobbled some, strutted some, and followed a hen around. Finally, they got quiet and went out of sight. Just when we were considering leaving, I saw them leave the ridge and march our direction. They appeared at 20 steps. I took one with an old paper Peters #4!

Kill 76 March 24, 2012 – Greene County (Cherokee Hollow)

Cherokee Hollow is a great place to start a season. Weirdest turkey season ever. March 15 opened with highs in the 70s, and every day of the season thus far (today is April 7) the high temps have been in the 70s and 80s. As such, the turkeys were gobbling early, all going good before the season began.

As usual, Dad and I found turkeys gobbling all around the bottom section the day before. They all went away. We then found turkeys gobbling later all around Twin Fields. They all went away too. So the next day, I went to the bottom section with Tripp, and Dad went to Twin Field. Tripp and I heard nothing and worked the entire bottom section slowly. It was a great day. Back at the four-wheeler, where we started the morning, I gave one last desperation yelp. A hen cut back at me in the woods, not too far. Tripp and I eased in about 50 yards and set up. She yelped back when suddenly a dude gobbled with her. He got going hot, answering every turkey noise I made. Suddenly, after 20 minutes, he was close. Tripp got still. The gobbler popped up out of the swamp at 50 yards running. I clucked to stop him at 20 steps, shot and missed. He got up and slowly started flying. I folded him. Then he got up again and ran to the right. I had a good shot and took him.

It was great and Tripp was with me. He kept talking for a day or two about how loud his gobble was. I'm glad he recognized that. I'm glad the turkey didn't get away. But my shooting concerns me. How do I miss turkeys like that? Really concerns me (see April 7, 2012 – a miss)

Miss 10 April 7, 2012 – Clay County
(Hollins Management Area)

This one hurts. I dug him out. Dug him out of Hollins. Nowhere close to a green field. Deep in the woods. Oh, how it hurts.

We were back in The Forest, after 25 years away. Dad started in The Forest, the Talladega National Forest, near Brent back in the 60s. I started with him there until I was about 12. Then we left The Forest for greener pastures with fewer hunters. And we got good. We killed a lot of turkeys over the next 25 years. Most on private land, some in hunting clubs, and a few on public land. But none were in The Forest. Many of the private places had pasture fields or green fields, some being bottom land, some being hill country – all were easier than working The Forest.

But our taste for the deep country bubbled up this year, so we mostly left the private lands to dig back into The Forest; this time Hollins, the separate tract of the Talladega National Forest near Sylacauga. And Hollins is awesome. I suspect a good percentage of turkeys killed in Hollins are on managed green fields, likely with decoys stuck in them. They are legal now, decoys that is, but we ain't gonna use 'em. Ain't right.

It has now been two weeks in Hollins. We found them gobbling good at first and developed a love/hate relationship with one turkey. During that time, he and all others just quit gobbling. While that has been frustrating, the landscape has been awe-inspiring. The majestic longleaf forests were burned just before season, making it the most aesthetically appealing forest I've ever hunted in. The forest floor has transformed from a charred barren expanse into a lush, deep carpet of ferns and grasses. It is mesmerizing.

Yesterday, we went deep into the woods after our boy only to flush him off roost. So we left and worked new areas. We found two separate turkeys gobbling far off the road, in a seemingly obscure area, but never could get close to them.

This morning, I went after them while Dad took Tripp to explore elsewhere. I made my way down a ridge in the dark, never having been on that ridge before, and listened overlooking the area where they'd been yesterday. One gobbled across the burn in unburned mixed hardwoods while dark. I closed fast. I set up below and they seemed to move up the ridge fast. It may have been three gobbling. I spent the next two hours working them lightly, closing in cautiously with four separate moves. Another hunter (we'll call him Mississippi) was on an adjacent ridge working them too. The turkeys gobbled well for the better part of an hour and a half. They moved around a little up the ridge and finally eased down a little closer. Their gobbling shut down to an every-10-minute affair. I kept my calling light as Mississippi was hitting a loud yelp every 10 minutes which always made them gobble. Mississippi was keeping their whereabouts known for me while I kept my calling subdued. It was perfect. I kept ready with my gun on my knee.

Either from discomfort or a chill, I suddenly began shaking uncontrollably and couldn't stop. After several minutes of this, I relaxed my legs and laid my gun down to gain composure. A minute later, a fan appeared around 30 yards in front of me. It folded down and he stood tall in plain view. I couldn't raise my gun and was so fearful he was looking at me and would spook. After a minute, he put his head down to eat and I got my gun up halfway. Then he stood tall again. Now I was holding my gun halfway up without my knees up to rest it on; and he stood tall for another minute or two. It was tortuous. Finally, he moved to the left when a separate turkey strutted behind him. They moved further left, eased behind a tree, and I got my gun all the way up. One stepped out the other side and craned his neck diagonally as if he was looking at me. Perhaps I panicked and didn't take a good shot. Perhaps I was so shook up that I just flat out missed. Maybe he pulled his head back just as I shot. Regardless, I missed and they flew quickly, one to the right, one to the left. My gun jammed to prevent a second shot. The hunter to my left shot at him five times as he flew over his position. He made it – thank God. I don't think I wounded him.

Shortly after the battalion of gunfire ended, the other hunter came up to talk. Only the hunter was actually three in company: two brothers from Sylacauga and south Mississippi with a young teenage son. We briefly ran through the events when a comical thing happened. Mississippi asked how long I'd been hunting. When I responded my whole life, he proceeded to berate my "awful" calling; he explained how terrible it was and how it ran the turkeys up towards them once. He hit the point several times, emphatic about conveying his opinion. It was as if he was offering strong rebuke for sinful ways that would tragically lead to death.

Ironically, while his rebuke certainly cut across the line of cordiality, it was I who had called the turkeys up. Just moments prior to his tongue lashing, I had whipped his tail and won the battle. I played the game at hand, utilized his loud yelps to keep the turkeys located, and called the turkeys in. What else can you say? If only I hadn't missed.

Kill 77 2013 – Coosa County (Cat Den)

I'm writing this a year later...

It was a cloudy and dreary morning, but we went anyway. We knew a pair had been gobbling deep in the Cat Den around the power line. We heard them while it was pretty dark across the power line. We set up near so that the power line would be about 30 yards away. They gobbled a few more times. Then it started drizzling rain. After 10 minutes of silence, they suddenly appeared in range in the power line. They moved slightly right and into our side of the woods. My gun wasn't up at first. I finally shouldered it and they got suspicious. I took a quick shot – missed. As he scrambled away, I missed two more times. Fortunately, the third shot knocked him down and he got up and came back into the woods, closer to me. I ran closer and shot him dead just as he was spreading his wings to fly.

Was fun but dreary and I missed on the first shot again. My shooting is suspect.

Kill 78 2013 – Coosa County (Cat Den)

I'm writing this a year later...

Dad and I heard nothing on Jade Fox from our usual spot. So we began road hunting. We finally heard one way down the mountain off Jade. So we went after him. We went down a long way, seeming to never get closer. It was thick. Finally, we set up. Lots of rocks and longleafs, and very thick. Finding a place to sit was difficult and the turkey would be on us before we saw him. He gobbled great – answered everything and came in slowly. I took him without Dad even knowing he was that close. It was great!

Kill 79 April 7, 2014 – Shelby County

Shelby County has changed recently. Turkey numbers have decreased substantially. And now, rules are in place that hunters must park and walk in from gates. So, our first hunt there of the season, Dad and I walked up to Jade Fox from Gate 5. It was a worthy effort, but unrewarding. Another day, we worked Gate 7. I found one near Slide Mountain (saw him on roost), but he went away (then we hiked up to top of mountain again – again, worthless). Dad and I found him again the next day and chased him about a mile (all turkeys go away these days). So another day came and we hunted all around Gate7 area looking for him. One last ditch effort, I climbed Slide Mountain to check the chamber. He answered my call not far away. I signaled to Dad below to come and quickly hit a tree. Dad came up within minutes, but I had to motion him to stop until I knew the turkey wasn't close. Within five minutes, I saw him coming – I took him with the old double Fox Sterlingworth and a blue Peters #6. It was good, but things have taken a downturn since…

I've closed the season with a never-before sense of despair and less joy than ever before. For two years now, we haven't made a turkey gobble after 9 o'clock. Furthermore, all turkeys go away on journeys, and gobblers mostly come in pairs akin to walking turkeys I described years ago in The Fire Tower. Turkey hunting is all about gobbling. Without gobbling, the affair is meaningless. Though we still hear turkeys gobble, they do it less consistently, are more often on journeys, and can't be worked like the old days. Take for example, the turkey I killed above. While it was good and enjoyable, one gobble and then kill him five minutes later is not the best. Perhaps it has been the weather. These past two years were very late springs. Both years, the woods looked like winter well into mid-April. Perhaps the hens never left the gobblers by season's end, and thus no turkey needed to gobble after 9 o'clock. Whatever the case, the season left Dad and me questioning our dedication to the pursuit. Dad has closed the past 10 or so seasons in such a state of mind, but never in such disgust as this one. And I closed my first season ever in such a state. I'm sure we will go again next year, but I'm not sure it is worth it. Maybe they will begin gobbling better. Maybe pairs will break up. Maybe the season will burst forth earlier. Maybe…

Kill 80 March 29, 2015 – Greene County (Cherokee Hollow)

The forest primeval is most epitomized to me by old growth bottomland such as where this story takes place. We arrived the day before for several days of hunting in the beautiful land. Day 1, Tripp and I called in turkeys two separate times, the second being a pair, but both times they were out of range. The pair came up in the most primordial of spots. I watched them work in from 200 yards out among the palmettos, gobbling and strutting some, only to flank us out of range. Since both groups were found in the same 20-acre area, I knew where we would be listening the next morning. Tripp and I walked in while it was very dark, getting all the way back to where I thought one or more would be roosting. Just as I started looking for a tree to listen by, in case he gobbled close, he did just that. Fortunately it was still dark as he couldn't have been more than 75 yards away. We set up and I gave only the lightest of yelps. He gobbled well with two others gobbling another 100 yards past. He flew down while still pretty dark, got silent for five minutes and resumed gobbling off with the other two now 200 yards away. So I worked them in with a little calling, first seeing them enter the back of that mysterious green field 150 yards out. They worked through the field then up the road to me, the back two gobbling and strutting often. I shot the lead and Tripp and I celebrated our first kill together in three years. Wow, it was awesome!

Miss 11 March 31, 2015 – Greene County (Cherokee Hollow)

I'd been in turkeys for three days at Cherokee Hollow, killing one with Tripp on the second day. I just knew a turkey would be roosting in the area I took Tripp. We worked through the woods while dark which was a good thing as it turned out we were covered up by gobbling turkeys once daylight hit. I found a tree to stand by (difficult to find a good tree in the dark) and a turkey gobbled no more than 50 yards away. We sat, wondering if he could see us and heard another within 100 yards directly behind us. The first turkey never gobbled again while the other gobbled well. I was too reluctant to spin knowing this turkey in front of us could easily fly down in range. He did eventually fly down though I never saw him. Heard others fly down with him too. That's when I should have spun to face the other turkey that was gobbling good behind me. But he eventually got silent for 10 minutes. and then gobbled close. Since I was over a slight rise, I spun a little his way and got awfully uncomfortable. He gobbled again (reassuring that I didn't spook) and got silent. Then I heard drumming moving to my right. I got left handed. It was getting close. I finally cut my eyes as far right as I could and saw him in range. I worked my gun over and up, but I was so twisted and uncomfortable that my vision was blurring in and out. With both eyes open I could see his head well (mostly strutting), but he mostly disappeared when I closed my right eye to aim the gun. Had I been comfortable and able to wait, I would have waited for a better shot. But I couldn't and finally pulled the trigger when I shouldn't have. I think I knocked him down but not sure. He ran off with me taking two desperation shots – never hitting him again. We looked for his dead body over the next three hours. Perhaps he lived.

Kill 81 April 9, 2015 – Coosa County (Hatchet Valley)

What a joy Hatchet Valley has been. We've found a new paradise. Turkeys it has, but the territory makes it. We forget how much terrain is in a thousand acres, and Hatchet Valley is 2,500 acres. We've been in turkeys all season. Dad killed one two weeks ago. We had hunted him three separate days.

Tripp and I called a great one in range for which I didn't pull the trigger (left handed – fearful after missing one two days before left handed). We also called another in who circled and popped his head up over a little mound not 10 yards away – he saw me instantly and split. All this to say the place has been productive. Lots of terrain to work and explore. So on the day at hand, Dad and I split. His morning only produced the climbing of giant ridges and getting lost.

I, on the other hand, heard turkeys everywhere but never close and I never got on one. I walked for two hours. Dad and I finally hooked back up and started chasing them around my area some more. Closest we got was a turkey just outside our signed-out territory. As we were about to sit and work him, we both heard a human owl hoot close by as if to say, "I'm on this turkey and you ought not to be here." So we split, taking a good hour to get out of the deep woods we were in. Upon signing back in, we saw that no one else had signed out for anywhere including the area we heard the mysterious and seemingly obvious human voice, "get out of here" owl hoot. My eyes lit up. I turned to Dad and said, "I know exactly where that turkey is and he will be easy to get to, only a short walk off a back road."

Dad said, "Let's go"! Just as I said, he was easy to find. We parked and walked a road through a thinned pine plantation. Dad sat by a tree near the start while I worked to the end of the road. But I didn't make it half-way. He gobbled near the end and I hit a tree quickly. He only gobbled that one time but must have started my way instantly. I yelped again a few times. Ten minutes later I heard drumming. Then I saw him easing through the thick woods at 75 yards towards the road I was sitting by. Predictably, he hit the road, strutted some and came my way strutting every few steps. Came just inside 29 yards before I pulled the trigger.

Kill 82 April 23, 2015 – Coosa County (Montane)

The pair. The pair. The damn pair. Well, the damn pair ain't no more!

I'm not sure how many years we've hunted the pair. Truth is, we've probably had many different pairs at Montane, not just the pair central to this story. Pairs are a phenomenon we've increasingly noticed in all places we hunt. Over the past 10 years, pairs have become the norm at Montane. And they've become common too at Cherokee Hollow and Clay County. The problem with pairs is that they are nearly impossible to call up. They usually gobble well, which is why we've hunted so many, but they all too often have premeditated journeys after flying down that leaves you trailing them in futility. Calling to them almost seems counterproductive. Get close to them and call and they'll shut up, move, and gobble somewhere else. Get in front of them, yelp, and they'll detour wide around you back to their premeditated journey.

The pair, the ones in this story, epitomized such behavior for two or more years, frustrating the hell out of us. But today was different. They finally came. But the whole affair opened and proceeded in fairly typical fashion. We heard them gobble at roost the night before behind the dogwood savannah. But as we approached them in the morning, they were actually across the creek and up in the park. They gobbled well, finally flew down, hushed for 10 minutes, and gobbled deeper in the park. We were on the wrong side of their movement again. So we split. Dad walked around the dam but could get no closer than Color Corner. I circled to the big savannah and up to the back of the park. I worked them in there for an hour with them moving towards the pasture. Dad finally circled around through the big savannah and up to the gate. He saw them out in the pasture moving towards the peninsula point. We met up, heard them gobble even farther away, now in the longleafs, and decided to run around by the lake and up to the woods knoll between the longleafs and road, a favorite place of theirs. Getting there fairly quickly, we heard them gobbling somewhere down in the middle of the longleafs. We had played it perfectly. We set up a couple different times in the woods but facing the field. Took about 30 minutes when they finally gobbled much closer, then closer again, then appeared up top walking fast. They followed the woods edge to my right where I took the lead with an old blue Peter's # 7 ½ in the Ithaca 16-gauge.

The pair is no more. We are the victors today

Miss 12 2016 – Coosa County (Hatchet Valley)

I'm writing this a year later and as such don't remember all the details…

Tripp turned 11 and dove hunted with the Ithaca double in the fall of 2015. He did well, and so I figured he was of age to shoot a turkey. We started the morning listening atop a ridge where my 10-year-old daughter, Juliet and I had two turkeys gobbling and fighting for the better part of two hours a week prior. We only heard one gobble a couple times way down the ridge, so we eventually went trolling. We eased up the road to Rattlesnake Ridge (that name didn't come until a year later, but I'm writing this a year later) and I made one gobble close to us. We jumped off the road to the right, found a good longleaf pine about 20 yards off the road, and made the turkey gobble again. He eventually hit the road, strutted and drummed a few times before coming to the edge of the road to look for us. Tripp had his gun up and aimed at the turkey when I whispered several times, "Shoot." Finally, he whispered back, "I don't want to." So I raised my gun, the turkey started to run, and I took a potluck shot without hitting him. I then took another long potluck shot with him flying away. Tripp was upset, fearful that I'd be mad. I wasn't and probably pushed him to shoot a turkey too soon. I have some guilt, though in truth he doesn't really have the hunting bug anyway. Lucky guy – wish I could shed my affliction.

Kill 83 2016 (middle of season) – Coosa County (Hatchet Valley)

Unfortunately I'm writing this story a year later, so I don't remember all the details…

Boy, this was a good one. Deep hardwoods, lots of gobbling – it just doesn't get much better. I had found a turkey a week earlier way down at the bottom of the Willis 50-acre area, in the hardwoods that connect to the back part. On this particular morning, a pair and another single turkey began gobbling a lot while near dark down across a creek and on top of a small ridge. I worked them for about an hour. They had hens with them, and after they flew down, it remained a lively affair as they moved to the right and nearer the creek bottom. They finally got far enough away that I jumped up, ran down and crossed the creek to their side. It was tough on that side with wide open hardwoods and little vegetation to hide. But they continued to go off and seemed to cross the creek to the other side. So I eventually slipped down their way to the tip of the ridge, near the conglomeration of creeks, and found quite a bit of green vegetation to hide me. I snuck up to a good pine tree, set up and called. One gobbled not too far away and some hens started yelping a bit closer to me. It lasted about 15 or 20 minutes with a few gobbles here and there before the gobbler appeared walking above me, right to left. I took him.

Miss 13 April 1, 2017 – Coosa County (Hatchet Valley)

As of early April, the 2017 season is evolving as in the old days. We opened in near silence, the woods barren and temperatures in the lower 20s on the second and third days. Ever so slowly, the gobbling increased to a fair amount by the end of March. We'd found a turkey early on, deep in the back hardwoods of the Willis tract, spent a week away for work and spring break, and returned at the end of March to find the gobbling quite lively. The first of five days in a row, we worked the turkey but he moved briskly and early off our ridge. Though we chased and eventually got on him close enough to hear drumming, he petered out after an hour or so.

Day 2, he did nearly the exact same thing but gobbled a lot more and for the better of two hours. We ended pretty close to him. In addition to hunting him, we heard others in the area.

On Day 3, we decided to beat him to the area he went to every morning, knowing he wouldn't do the exact same thing three days in a row, which is exactly what happened. Had we started on the same ridge as the two previous mornings, he'd have walked right by us.

Day 4, things exploded. Turkeys started gobbling while it was dark, in fact while we were getting out of the truck, and continued for three hours. The turkey we moved in on, the one we'd hunted three mornings before, gobbled the least of all five that we heard. We hung with him for the better part of 1 ½ hours when Dad slipped away to go after one gobbling his head off near the truck. In such typical fashion, soon as Dad left, he never gobbled again. When Dad finally returned, all the turkeys had pretty much shut up. So we went walking down Rattlesnake Ridge and agreed to split and meet back at the truck. Not long after, he texted me that a turkey was gobbling good his direction. I finally went his way, surprised how far he had gone in such a short period of time. The turkey was on the goat trail side of the Willis Loop road. I eventually met up with Dad, and we eased up the road a good bit closer. He was gobbling real good.

We set up at the same tree with Dad aiming down the open hardwoods and the direction that we thought he'd come from. I was aimed left into thicker woods and knew if he came my way, he'd be close by the time I saw him. It took about 10 minutes, but he responded to our calls and shut up when he came except for one gobble halfway. And then he appeared in front of me, close as expected, walking fast right to left. With no big trees for him to walk behind and hide my movement, I got my gun up as his head went behind a small tree. He saw me, kind of, and stopped walking briefly to look. But he then put his head down and started walking again. I didn't have a good shot, though he was close, and shot more out of desperation before he got away. Only his head and neck were visible over a rise, so when I shot, he instantly disappeared. I don't think I knocked him down, though I'm not sure about that, and by the time I ran up to find him, he was flying off from a good 20 yards away. I took another potluck wing shot, missed again, and watched him soar far away. I can only hope he lived. We went over and scoured the woods he flew to, never did find him, and so I think he lived unwounded. It would have been a great end to an incredible four-day stretch of classic deep hardwoods hill country hunting.

We went back the next day and they all stayed quiet. Strange creatures they are!

Kill 84 April 7, 2017 – Coosa County (Hatchet Valley)

Whew. After Dad and I both missed a turkey each this season, it was good to score. This turkey wasn't the best in terms of amount of gobbling or number of days we hunted him, but we earned him and he died honorably.

We worked the deep hardwoods in the back of the Willis tract surprised to find only one gobbling in the back. We worked him for an hour or so with one past him, across Hatchet creek gobbling his head off. They finally quit and so we journeyed along the horse path to the other area off Willis Road (with all the green fields). Working towards the top of a road, one answered my yelp fairly close. We hit the woods to our right, set up 10 yards off the road and stared through thick vegetation at the road, knowing that if he came, it would probably be along the road and he would be very close when we saw him. After five minutes, he gobbled a lot closer. A couple minutes after that, I heard him drum on top of me and then he appeared, walking right to left. I took him at 13 steps. Thank God I didn't miss another.

Dad and I prayed and thanked the Lord for the blessing! It was a beautiful, crisp, sunny and still morning.

That's what it's all about.

Kill 85 March 31, 2018 – Greene County (Cherokee Hollow)

We started the first of two days, March 30 and 31, amongst five gobbling turkeys roosting over a swamp with hens yelping and cutting in and around the swamp too. They all flew down, split into a couple groups, and moved about the woods fairly close but out of sight. The more vocal of the two groups moved off a bit and back again, and a pair among them gobbled their heads off until one of the gobblers in their group broke off and came in alone. Dad shot him 45 minutes into the operation. It was an awesome experience in a densely shaded, hardwood bottomland with fluorescent greens carpeting the forest floor splattered with to two to three-foot tall yellow-top.

As good of a hunt as that morning was, the next day's hunt was even better. Most of it was spent with a pair that gobbled at everything for three hours in the company of a third gobbler who stayed a little to himself and didn't gobble at all. We knew this because the back half of the operation took place in sight of each other, though they mostly stayed over a 100 yards out, moving away and back again through the open bottomland. I'm sure we watched them as far out as 200 yards at one point. It was that darn loner that was our downfall. He spent much of his time standing in one spot, standing tall, looking for us intently while his underlings roamed about in full sexual lust. They gobbled at sparrows and crows and us and any sound they could use as an excuse to exercise their lungs. And when they finally did come in, the loner led the charge, though it was more of a creep than a charge. He stopped in sight, 100 yards out, then 50, then 40, and stood for minutes on end each time looking intently for us. He got to a point where he might have been just in range, gave a few putts to hush everyone up and they all moved off. We didn't pull a trigger. I could have pulled the trigger and almost did. And I probably should have. I had a chance to but was afraid. I was afraid because while I can brag about being a really good shot on the dove field, as I said before, I'm absolutely terrible at shooting turkeys. I miss turkeys far more often than I should, and the problem seems to be getting worse.

The miss a year prior did it for me. I finally admitted to the fact that I had a problem. It was like I had a come-to-Jesus meeting with repentance in full swing. The details of the miss included a great call-up in deep, hilly hardwoods which I ruined by taking a poor shot. Then again, maybe it wasn't a poor shot and I was just a poor shooter. But the heartbreaking miss got me to honestly evaluate how to shoot turkeys so much that I even practiced with several boxes of low brass shells over the offseason.

You see, I think I flinch. It's kind of embarrassing to admit, but I think I do. I know I do as such when patterning a gun. I don't know how not to when sitting there squeezing the trigger and knowing you are about to be hammered by a magnum shell with only a piece of cardboard to distract you. Two and three quarter-inch shells hit you hard whereas 3 ½-inch magnums are just plain sick. I'd always figured that while I flinched when patterning and shooting a target, I was so caught up in the moments of calling up real turkey that I wouldn't succumb to such cowardice and flinch when pulling the trigger. But Dad somewhat proved that theory wrong when years ago he squeezed the trigger on a gobbler only to find the safety on. And he flinched. He flinched so bad that the significant movement of his body and gun could have scared the turkey away. Fortunately it didn't and he got the safety off and killed the turkey. After missing that turkey last year, I actually remember flinching which undoubtedly threw my aim off. The turkey was only 20 yards away. How else do you explain it?

So after 10 ½ months off the battle ground contemplating my tendency to miss turkeys, I didn't pull the trigger on a great looking gobbler who may have been in range because I was afraid of missing him. I'm not totally at fault here. He was working in, albeit slowly, so I figured it was best to let him close a few more yards, thus making the shot more certain. But we were in wide open bottomland with little cover around us. He got just close enough to see us and I missed a great opportunity to kill a majestic gobbler in a majestic wood, though letting him walk was better than missing him.

After the loner and his underlings moved off, we headed across the property to find another. And find another or two we did. We got two separate turkeys gobbling immediately along with a very vocal jake who worked our direction slowly, eventually strolling behind us at 75 yards with a hen. Since neither of the gobbling turkeys followed, and since it had been an hour or so of action, we decided to move a little closer to one of the two. We only had to go about 100 yards before hitting a strange ridge. It was only 15 feet tall but seemed strangely out of place in this bottomland habitat. We almost topped the ridge before I got nervous and made us set up barely seeing the top woods instead of presenting ourselves more openly at the top and spooking the turkey should he happen to be closer than we thought. It wasn't three minutes before he, though it was a pair and not a single, gobbled not 50 yards in front of us. They gobbled another two times somewhat to the right, not in sight, so I switched my gun and got ready left handed. Then I saw their fans and they turned and started working back to the left, stopping to strut and gobble a few times. They presented themselves in an opening now slightly to my left, perhaps in range though perhaps not, and I was now in an awkward left handed position trying to aim left of center. I'd already let a turkey go once today, which may have been the right decision, but I wasn't going to let another.

Such moments of decision-making before pulling the trigger are often chaotic at best. I remember simultaneously considering that they may be in range, but maybe not, that I was in a precarious shooting position, that they had stopped walking and seemed to be staring at me as if I were naked. Furthermore the two turkeys were close to each other, and I didn't want to kill both with one shot, or worse, kill one and incidentally wound the other. After taking all these considerations to mind within a matter of half a second, I pulled the trigger – AND MISSED!

I can shoot doves, not turkeys.

The immediate moments after shooting a gobbler are much like the immediate moments just before; chaotic at best, especially if you miss. It always takes me a second to regain my bearings after being jolted backwards by the recoil. The turkey often disappears, either having fallen onto the forest floor hidden by brush, or rises in the terrain, or sometimes already running or flying away. I knew I'd missed when I heard Dad shoot before I saw a dead or live turkey. I then saw one flying away to my left and another running angled away to my right. I took a potluck shot at the one running, figuring he was the one I missed, perhaps even wounded though at this point I didn't know. I'm pretty sure I hit nothing. I took off running as Dad expended another shell and took another long shot as the turkey kept running through the woods. He made his way to the edge of a field with me in a full-out sprint perhaps 30 yards behind. I figured at this point he must be wounded because he'd have easily run or flown out of sight at this point had he been able. I entered the field and saw him turn down a side road back into the woods now only 20 yards away. I rounded the corner to the road and saw him semi-flopping but head upright and looking at me as I ran closer. He hopped up, half ran another five yards into the woods and I put another round into him. That did it and I took him home. Thank God he didn't become wildcat meat.

It was a day God intended for turkey hunting; sunny and cool, not cold, nearly breathless all day, gorgeous bottomland hardwoods exploding in various fluorescent greens and yellow-top splattering the scene, turkeys gobbling all day with mixed joys and despairs – all in the company of a great hunting friend.

Kill 86 April 3, 2018 – Chilton County (Hillcrest Hunting Club)

It wasn't the most exciting, but I dug him out. On new property that I'd never even seen, I walked in the backside of Round Rock just hoping to find some huntable territory. Google Earth images showed the entire property to be pine plantation, not the most enjoyable turkey territory. I made one gobble far off at first light and eased down a road in his direc-tion. Once a train passed, I made him gobble again fairly close. I eased down further then entered the woods only to find briars in every direction. I made a mental note never to enter the woods here again. To make mat-ters worse, he wasn't gobbling anymore. I finally worked out of the bramble jungle and worked a road to find I was going away from the turkey. So I doubled back to where he gobbled the second time and took the other fork in the road. About 300 yards down the road, I rounded a corner and saw a hen standing in the road, her back to me, not 25 yards away. I froze and she didn't move either. I could see her head and neck craned out to the side as if she was staring at me. But she didn't move a muscle for so long that I wondered if she was somebody's decoy. I even took out my phone to text Dad the situation. After a couple minutes, I finally moved out in the open a bit more and she flew. The road ahead ventured straight down for over a hundred yards to where the turkey had gobbled an hour earlier, though I didn't step out far enough to see all the way down. Knowing the woods weren't walkable, and having just spooked a hen up here, I figured this was a good set up to call the gobbler up the road. I found a tree five yards off the road, yelped, and he gobbled a 100 yards down the road. A little more yelping and two more gobbles confirmed the game was on. Ten minutes into the operation I heard him drumming close. At 15 steps with lots of brush between us, I took him. I carried him out under glory though it was short lived. I met the "asshole" back at my truck. [I really don't want to get into this, but it would be unfair to readers to leave the topic unexplained. I had parked at a gate entering the hunting club property because my key didn't work. I later found out the key didn't work because we weren't supposed to enter the property through that gate at all. Several years before, it was a main access until a new landowner forbid driving across his property to the gate. But I didn't know that because I had joined the club just three weeks before the season opened and never had a chance to meet up with the club huntmaster for a drive-around and tour. So upon finding my truck parked at the gate, the landowner called the police and made due on a promise to prosecute any club member driving across his property to get into the club through that gate. I was that lucky soul. After apologizing many times to the landowner and accepting my ticket from the officer, I called the huntmaster with my tail between my legs to detail my misgivings for which he reacted sympathetically that I been caught up in nonsense and that in short, the landowner was an asshole and everyone in the county knew it. The case was later dismissed at the court hearing, and two days later, the landowner was pushed out as principal of the local high school.]

Kill 87 March 28, 2019 – Greene County (Cherokee Hollow)

Wow. What a turkey. Huge – 24 lbs. My best spurs ever – 1-½".

And what a day. Dad killed one early after we worked a pair for an hour with many gobbling around us. His came up deep in the bottom area circling a small swamp. And he was big, we think 21 ½ pounds.

After relishing the kill, taking a break and talking Arthur [caretaker of the property] into cleaning him, we headed to the back part of the property where we've found many turkeys in the mid-mornings. We eased in and up to where I killed one last year. This time however, nothing gobbled. We set up and called for a while. Dad laid down to nap. After 30 minutes or so, I left to troll the roads above the fields leaving Dad to rest some more. I trolled up and around for 20 minutes when one answered me 200-300 yards off. I set up and didn't say another word. In 10 minutes he worked almost straight in, stopping to semi-strut a few times. Because he was angling to my right, I got ready left handed. Finally, he was close enough. I yelped to stop his walking and pulled the trigger.

Kill #88 April 5, 2019 – Coosa County (Golf Course)

Wow. Finally killed one around the golf course. We don't know what it is about that golf course, but turkeys love it. And now that it's closed, they have unfettered access to roam its terrain. The day before, Dad and I worked a gobbling loner in the middle of the back end while the trio which we've been chasing around everywhere strutted with eight hens 100 yards away. None of them paid us any attention. We eventually gave up on them.

Morning came and I got to the back green before cracking time. I played my cards perfectly as he gobbled about 200 yards out in the cutover and while it was dark enough for me to move around to the other side of the green. He gave me a courtesy gobble after to let me know I hadn't spooked him. He gobbled a couple more times before a few hens out his way started yelping. I eventually heard some fly down and caught occasional glimpses of hens walking around in the cutover 150 yards out. He finally gobbled again, closer, and a little to my right. I got ready left handed. One more gobble announced he was coming when I saw him marching in slightly flanking to the left. I got on him and he got close quick. Dad heard me shoot from Montane knowing I scored!

Miss 14 April 2, 2019 – Bibb County

What a bone-headed mistake...

I spent the previous two months analyzing all my kills and misses finding that misses were correlated with higher powered guns with tighter chokes. So today I took the Fox with two paper Peters shells.

A pair gobbled early down in the woods while I was still walking. I found a hidden place to sit 200 yards away. They gobbled like mad at everything. I eventually heard them fly down. They shut up and I saw them 100 yards out moving fast to my right. I called a little. One came. He hit the road to my right just over a rise perhaps 40 yards. He hung there for a few minutes gobbling and strutting, then left walking away down the road. I called a little more. In another few minutes I heard them walking up the ridge and to my right. I spun a little and got ready left handed. He gobbled close. Then I saw them, perhaps 40 yards out. I waited. One gobbled and strutted again. The non-gobbling turkey worked down the ridge to an open area. He looked close, so I clucked to stop his walking and pulled the modified trigger with a paper Peters #4. That was the mistake. Later patterning showed a wide open pattern. At 35 yards with those old #4's, I didn't have a chance. Indeed he ran off unscathed. I could only hope he wasn't wounded.

Addendum – see April 8, 2019 story. He lived!!!!

Kill #89 April 8, 2019 – Bibb County

Well, it wasn't such a bad thing that I missed a week before. I figured and hoped he wasn't wounded – and he wasn't. The same pair both gobbled fairly early down in there, but I had walked past them. So I ran back up the road a ways and eased half-way up the ridge. They were gobbling good. I set up being able to see fairly far. Just as last week, they gobbled at everything. A hen started yelping 100 yards off center to my left and between us. I figured I was dead. But I heard them fly down and eventually saw them working my way but angling to my right. I got ready left handed. They had quit gobbling on the move just like last week. The lead turkey approached at 35 yards, flanking my position giving me one window for a shot, but it was poor so I passed to wait on the other. The other lagged a little bit, gobbled and strutted before easing by the same shooting window. I passed on it too – just too risky. He proceeded on behind me at 45 yards so that I was now twisted in a most uncomfortable left handed shooting position. He stayed there gobbling and strutting for 10 minutes while the other hung around another 20 yards out. I lightly called to work him back in, certain that he'd follow the other on further out. But he eventually turned and worked back my way gobbling and strutting until he was in the same shooting window as before. But I still didn't shoot because it seemed a little too far. My patience paid off. He worked in another five steps and I pulled the trigger. Had I killed that turkey last week, this experience probably wouldn't have happened, and it was Awesome!!!!

Kill #90 April 21, 2019 – Coosa County (Cat Den)

Wow. This one was awesome. Easter morning. Dad was sick and stayed home. Prompted by Kathy, I took both kids despite Tripp not really wanting to go. But they went in the spirit of tradition. I woke them at 3:50 to dress and we set out at 4:00. They slept almost the whole way, waking briefly to place orders for powdered donuts, chocolate and strawberry milk, and a pop tart from the convenience store. We got to the blueberry bushes early, planning to walk across and hunt the golf course. Since they were still sleeping, I was able to get out and hide their Easter baskets.

We listened across the GC and heard one gobble back towards the truck, probably past it somewhere on the edge of the golf range/field. Nothing gobbled where we were, so we made our way to the island in the GC, set up and began working a pair who were gobbling well – as if they would come our way and cross the paved road.

Finally, because they were gobbling so well, I led us around to and past the back tee box, across the road and into the cat den. They gobbled the whole way and were out in the field near the first power line pole. We eased up in the woods towards the corner of the power line until I spotted them 150 yards out.

We set up at a small tree with Juliet facing behind so she wouldn't have to see me shoot one while Tripp hunkered down to my left with his hood pulled over his face. The pair gobbled well until a separate single gobbler across the power line started gobbling his head off and worked up and into the power line. The pair shut up. The single hung up there, perhaps 75 yards away hidden by the brush. He proceeded to gobble at everything for the next 30 minutes. Tripp fell asleep for a while which wasn't a bad thing because he was still. Then he woke and got fidgety asking over and over when this would be over.

I quit calling the last 15 minutes in hopes the turkey would either come on in or leave so Tripp wouldn't have to sit there longer. The turkey finally got quiet so I knew he was on the move. A gobble finally came from the field but seemingly closer than where I had seen the pair. Was it him or the pair? After another couple of silent minutes, I decided to take a look. I slowly stood up and saw the pair strutting in the same spot. I was in the process of telling the kids they could st and and watch the turkeys when the single gobbled in the power line but obviously closer. Now I was now standing up like a fool and he was close. I got down and set quickly. He gobbled again closer. He appeared shortly after coming in front of Tripp. It was wide open there. But I was on him and had a great shot. The new TSS #9 did their business at 34 yards. Both the kids were surprised at the whole affair and happy for me. Juliet helped carry him out. Back at the truck, they found their Easter baskets hanging in the blueberry bushes and were amazed. It was a great Easter morning. Thank you, God!

A special thanks to Julie Coolidge for graciously devoting much of her time and talents editing this book.

www.ingramcontent.com/pod-product-compliance
Lightning Source LLC
Chambersburg PA
CBHW041258040426
42334CB00028BA/3068